ANGLO-AMERICAN UNION

ANGLO-AMERICAN UNION

UNION

Joseph Galloway's

PLANS TO PRESERVE

THE BRITISH EMPIRE

1774-1788

By

JULIAN P. BOYD

1970

OCTAGON BOOKS

New York

Reprinted 1970

by special arrangement with the University of Pennsylvania Press

OCTAGON BOOKS

A DIVISION OF FARRAR, STRAUS & GIROUX, INC.
19 Union Square West
New York, N. Y. 10003

Reproduced from a copy in the Yale University Library

LIBRARY OF CONGRESS CATALOG CARD NUMBER: 76-120233

Printed in U.S.A. by
NOBLE OFFSET PRINTERS, INC.
NEW YORK 3, N. Y.

To

CARL VAN DOREN

*whose understanding of men and motives
of the American Revolution
is as great, and as generously shared,
as his friendship and his encouragement.*

CONTENTS

ACKNOWLEDGMENT

Two of the manuscripts of Joseph Galloway's Plans of Union reproduced in this volume are owned by Mr. Lawrence J. Morris of Philadelphia, who has graciously permitted me to publish them. A scholar and a collector, Mr. Morris has placed me under immense obligation by lending some of Galloway's pamphlets from his library, by showing a constant interest in the progress of my research, and by generously providing that essential element which publishers insist upon for books of this sort. I acknowledge this obligation with genuine pleasure, being impressed once more with the benefits conferred upon scholarship by discriminating collectors. While Mr. Morris has an intimate knowledge of Joseph Galloway's career, and has generously shared that knowledge with me, he should not be held responsible for my interpretation of Galloway's ideas or of the rôle of the conservative in the American Revolution. That, of course, is my own responsibility.

I am likewise indebted to the scholarly writings of Adams, Coupland, McIlwain, Mullett, and Schuyler on the political and constitutional aspects of the Revolution. To Dr. Randolph G. Adams, Director of the William L. Clements Library, for permission to publish the Plans of Union addressed to Lord George Germain; to Dr. St. George L. Sioussat, Chief of the Division of Manuscripts of the Library of Congress, for permission to publish the unaddressed Plan of Union drawn up about 1785; and to Mr. Alexander J. Wall, Director of the New York Historical Society, for permission to publish the slightly variant copy of the Plan of Union of 1774, I wish also to express my particular gratitude. Professors Alpheus T. Mason and Malcolm O. Young of Princeton University, Dr. Max Farrand, Director of The Henry E. Huntington Library, Dr. John H. Powell of Iowa State College, Mr.

ACKNOWLEDGMENT

Howard Peckham of the William L. Clements Library, and Dr. Victor H. Paltsits of the New York Public Library have likewise benefited me by their helpful suggestions and generous assistance. I wish particularly to express my sense of obligation to Dr. Raymond C. Werner for permission to make use of the typescript of his doctoral dissertation entitled "Joseph Galloway: His Life and Times" (University of Iowa, 1927) which has proved exceedingly useful.

JULIAN P. BOYD

Princeton University
April 1, 1941

INTRODUCTION

IF LEARNING, industry, and attention are guarantees, the American Revolution ought to be one of the best understood movements in history. Historians have explored its immediate and remote causes, its economics and its politics, its personalities and its motives, its local and its imperial aspects. They have broken the great movement up into tight little compartments as a physicist might reduce the mystery of light to its spectral components. They have explained the impact of the West on British imperial policy and on colonial acquisitiveness. They have examined the system of the Navigation Acts as a possible source of friction. They have probed into the activities and attitudes of the colonial merchants. They have thrown light on quit-rents and systems of land tenure as potential grievances. They have pored over countless ledgers and account books in appraising the influence of debts owed by Americans to London houses as a factor in determining loyalties. They have examined the social consequences of the Revolution. They have described the antipathy existing between classes and between sections as another contributory cause. They have analyzed the importance of religion in welding or dividing allegiances. They have lately investigated its mechanism of propaganda, organized by an articulate minority to influence attitudes. They have explored, and are still exploring, the misty realm of political and constitutional theory of the Revolution.

This account of Joseph Galloway's several Plans of Union, drawn up at various times between 1774 and 1788 to provide an imperial constitution which would prevent the threatened disintegration of the British Empire, is another fragment of the constitutional history of the American Revolution. But one who deals in fragments must perpetually face the question of relating the parts to the whole. Have we really under-

stood the American Revolution better by acquiring all possible information about its fragments? Is it not possible that
by throwing the spotlight upon the frictions caused by a
smuggled cargo or a few shillings in quit-rents or some thou-
sands of acres of wilderness land we have thereby thrown
into relative darkness the central fact of the Revolution? Has
it not been too often the case that those who examined with
scholarly care the writings of the leaders of the Revolution
on the nature of government and the rights of man have regarded those political ideals as, at best, incongruous ration-
alizations unrelated to facts, and, at worst, as protective logic
for sordid self-interest? Is it possible that historians, fully
conscious of the violence done those political ideals by nine-
teenth-century exploitation, have read their own generation's
disintegrating convictions into the Revolutionary leaders'
minds, endowing them with an exaggerated concern for
lands, debts, fisheries, and illicit trade? Is it possible that in
the light of our unbelief in political ideals belied by facts, in
the light of our distrust of slogans skilfully manipulated, in
the light of our skepticism of motives, historians of the Age
of Reason have too much reflected the cynicism of the Age
of Disillusion? In short, have we forgotten—or are we re-
membering only under the false compulsion of fear?—that,
whatever petty tyrannies or small ambitions or unworthy
self-interests it may have cloaked, the American Revolution
is profoundly important because it was the expression of an
ancient human hope?

Dr. Richard Price, an Englishman and a true disciple of the
Age of Reason, expressed that hope in his *Observations on
the Importance of the American Revolution, and the Means
of Making it a Benefit to the World.* "Perhaps I do not go too
far," he wrote at the conclusion of the Revolution, "when I
say that, next to the introduction of Christianity among mankind, the American revolution may prove the most important
step in the progressive course of human improvement." It
will be noted, of course, that Dr. Price was a contemporary,

in a sense a participant, and that he therefore lacked that time-perspective and objectivity which the historian insists are necessary for the correct appraisal of events. Worse, he believed in progress. Despite these limitations, he advanced some interesting observations in support of his broad generalization. First, the British themselves, if they properly understood and applied the meaning of the American Revolution, would become its chief beneficiary. Second, the American Revolution was an enormous catalyst. It brought the aristocrat and the yeoman, the conservative and the radical, the wealthy and the poor, to the common ground of reflecting upon the nature of government, the rights of mankind, the sovereignty and the obligations of the individual in society. Opinions on these broad concepts clashed violently, but at least there was reading and reflection about them: a welter of pamphlets, broadsides, and newspaper essays offered opinions as diverse as those of Blackstone and Adam Smith, of Lord Mansfield and Dean Tucker, of John Wesley and Samuel Adams. Third, even in the midst of invasion and war, the American states had erected their own forms of government based on the broad principle "that all legitimate government consists in the dominion of equal laws made with common consent; that is, in the dominion of men over *themselves*; and not in the dominion of communities over communities, or of any men over other men." Finally, and greatest of all, the success of the Revolution permitted these governments to live and to continue to give expression to the principles on which they were founded. America, then, became the hope of the future "by providing, in a sequestered continent, possessed of many singular advantages, a place of refuge for oppressed men in every region of the world; and by laying the foundation there of an empire which may be the seat of liberty, science and virtue, and from whence there is reason to hope these·sacred blessings will spread, till they become universal, and the time arrives when kings and priests shall have no more power to oppress, and that ig-

[3]

nominious slavery which has hitherto debased the world is exterminated."

The obscure colonial merchant who, on the day before the Stamp Act was to go into effect, wrote into his journal "The Last Day of Liberty" was only trying to say what Dr. Price said much more explicitly. How, then, can objective scholarship and the scientific method deal with a human hope? "The Revolution was in the minds and hearts of the people; a change in their religious sentiments of their duties and obligations," wrote John Adams. Too often historians, unable to prove it, have tacitly denied the presence and the power of such an intangible. The Age of Enlightenment was one that developed strong convictions; and belief in the inalienable rights of life, liberty, and property, in religious freedom, in freedom of the press, in freedom of speech, in equality before the law, gave meaning and dignity to the lives of the obscure and the conspicuous alike. "This House," wrote the speaker of the Virginia House of Burgesses in 1768, "hope they have Expressed Themselves on this Occasion with a ffirmness that Becomes free men pleading for fundamental rights." Belief in rights that were fundamental to human dignity produced inevitably "a ffirmness that Becomes free men." Nor did these beliefs belong solely to the eighteenth century: their history was more than two thousand years old. Nor did they belong solely to the Anglo-Saxon heritage. Nor did they belong solely to the literate: the consent of the governed was a concept that the merchant in Virginia or the artisan in Philadelphia or the Green Mountain boy in Vermont could respond to as firmly as a Jefferson or an Adams.

It might be argued, in fact, that the strength of a conviction is in inverse ratio to literacy. "When . . . Mr. Locke's *Essay on the human Understanding* was first published in Britain," so Dr. Price contended, "the persons readiest to attend to it and to receive it were those who had never been trained in colleges; and whose minds, therefore, had never been perverted by an instruction in the jargon of the schools."

[4]

The conservatism of such men as Joseph Galloway, Samuel Seabury, and Charles Inglis may have been due not merely to the fact that their interests were threatened by the democratic spirit, not merely to the fact that subversive forces were undermining an acceptable order of society, but also to their intellectuality which, in the face of an ancient and apparently insoluble problem of government, denied the possibility of ardent partisanship or unshakable convictions of right or wrong. "Almost all of the people of heart and spirit are in the rebellion," remarked Lord Howe in December 1776. What Galloway and other conservatives did not understand was that beliefs in human rights were not less ardently believed, or not less fiercely defended, because those beliefs were sometimes betrayed or because they were sometimes debased to serve unworthy ends or because their believers were sometimes without property, without social position, or without an intellectual acquaintance with the great writers on government. The important thing about the American Revolution, which the conservative mind overlooked, was not that Parliament was more stupid than tyrannical, not that the English yeoman was less free than the American farmer, but that American farmers and merchants and clergymen and land speculators and shopkeepers and artisans believed with an ardent and consuming belief that their freedom was threatened.

The problem of Galloway, therefore, is the enduring problem of the conservative intellect when faced with profound social forces which threaten the rigidity of established institutions. The doctrine of Parliamentary supremacy, buttressing the repressions and restrictions of a philosophy of empire which regarded colonies in terms of pounds sterling, was challenged by three million colonists who had grown too strong to suffer real or even imaginary restrictions. Such a challenge to the existing order could not be met by the placid logic of a Galloway, a Mansfield, or a Blackstone with its devotion to what George III called "the beauty, the ex-

[5]

cellence, and perfection of the British constitution as by Law established." If, as Galloway thought, the American appeal to natural law cloaked the ambitions and self-interests of a small group of demagogic leaders trying to bring the colonists into sedition and rebellion, it might with equal force be said that the British appeal to the excellences of the British constitution covered the narrow aims of a Mercantilist conception of empire. When the British Parliament clung blindly to the proposition that it "had, hath, and of right ought to have full power and authority to make laws and statutes of sufficient force and validity to bind the colonies and people of America, subjects of the Crown of Great Britain, in all cases whatsover," it may have had on its side, as Galloway and many American historians believed, the weight of legal authority. By so doing, it saved the cherished principle of Parliamentary supremacy, but it lost the richest part of the empire and dug the grave of the Mercantilist system. It was not the first time, nor the last, that those who championed the established system against the hard facts of social growth wagered the past against the future.

Perhaps no one of his generation in America or in England sacrificed more or labored more assiduously to compromise the uncompromisable issue than Galloway. His effort, if blind to reality, was characterized by a sort of noble stubbornness, as the efforts of the conservative so often are. He was fully conscious of the immense import of the issue and frequently described it as the most solemn one ever to be decided by a nation. He firmly believed that the empire was doomed if it lost a third of its population, the greater part of its territory, and a large proportion of its total commerce. "It does not seem to require more than a plain understanding to perceive," he wrote in reply to the Dean of Gloucester, "that while the other powers in Europe shall retain those nurseries of people, those sources of industry, commerce, wealth, and power, it will not only be sound policy, but absolutely necessary for Great Britain, *in order to preserve her*

[6]

independence among nations, to retain in like manner her Colonies in due subordination." He was not alone in this belief. "The moment that the independence of America is agreed to by our Government," declared Lord Shelburne, "the sun of Great Britain is set, and we shall no longer be a powerful or respectable people." Horace Walpole, in England's blackest moment, found no ground for confidence anywhere and declared that "We shall moulder piecemeal into our insignificant islandhood." But, just as dismemberment of the empire, the threat of national bankruptcy, and the hostile combination of European nations seemed about to destroy England, the threat of ruin shocked her people into resolute action and gave them renewed courage.

Thus by her disaster England became a beneficiary of the American Revolution. It gave impetus to her own Parliamentary reform, it ended the personal system of government of George III, but most of all it gave solemn warning to British statesmen that an empire bound together by force and the old narrow conceptions of the functions of colonies was no longer possible. A century and a half later, the principles of the imperial constitution defended by Benjamin Franklin, James Wilson, Thomas Jefferson, and John Adams triumphed in a free association of equals within the empire. It would not be too much to say that the shadow of America's Revolutionary leaders fell across the Statute of Westminster in 1931.

As for America, she was left free to work out her own destiny. Her leaders who had challenged the sovereignty of Parliament found themselves faced at once with the same problem: "I do not conceive," wrote George Washington, "we can exist long as a nation without having lodged somewhere a power, which will pervade the whole Union in as energetic a manner as the authority of the State governments extends over the several States." The solution to this problem was the great, triumphant achievement of the Age of Reason: the work of the Federal Convention of 1787. If by her separation from the empire America denied herself the advantages of the imperial relation, the success of her own political institutions received no higher tribute than the contrasts between Canada and the United States that formed the underlying refrain of the most important state document in imperial history, the *Durham Report*.

Though Joseph Galloway's self-sacrificing loyalty to an idea and his futile persistence in advocating compromise command our respect, Americans and Englishmen alike have reason to congratulate themselves that Dr. Richard Price was a better prophet.

CHAPTER I

THE MIDDLE DOCTRINE

"BY WHAT MEANS," asked Lord North, "is authority to be maintained but by Establishing that Authority from Parliament?"[1] His colleagues in Parliament knew that the question was rhetorical, and it took more than a century of development in imperial control to provide an acceptable answer. A few American writers, led by James Wilson, Thomas Jefferson, and John Adams, had already given the answer in their able publications. But since that answer denied the authority that Lord North symbolized, the statesmen of Whitehall saw it not as rational theory but as rebellion. Inasmuch as governments are conducted by human beings, a political theory must be more than merely plausible, reasonable, or even just to impress itself upon responsible statesmen: it must coincide with the national mores, with the pressure of events upon institutions, with the warnings of past experiences. The political climate in which Lord North moved was one which, with all its faults, was kind to English institutions: the commerce of the empire passed through English ports, creating wealth at home without depriving distant colonies of too much; East Indian nabobs and West Indian planters and British manufacturers talked of "*our* colonies" and "*our* plantations" in the comforting knowledge that the British navy would keep the bonds of empire firm; and at Oxford Sir William Blackstone gave, in solemn language, the expected answer to Lord North's question. "There is and must be in every state," Blackstone declared, "a supreme, irresistible, absolute, uncontrouled authority, in which the *jura summi imperii*, or the rights of sovereignty reside . . . this supreme power is, by the Constitution of Great Britain, vested in the

[1] W. Baring Pemberton, *Lord North* (London, 1938), 200.

[9]

King, Lords, and Commons . . . therefore, the . . . Acts of Parliament have, by the British Constitution, a binding force on the American Colonies, they composing a part of the British Empire."[2]

But the climate of commerce, settlement, western lands, town meetings, and free presses had been preparing a different answer in British North America since 1607. When England began her reorganization of colonial administration in 1763, the answer was hesitant, groping, and entertained by few. Benjamin Franklin was one of the few, though he was not dogmatic:

The more I have thought on the subject the more I find myself confirmed in opinion that no middle doctrine can be well maintained, I mean not clearly and with intelligible arguments. Something might be made of either of the extremes: that Parliament has a right to make all laws for us, or that it has a power to make *no laws* for us; and I think the arguments for the latter are more numerous and weighty than those for the former.[3]

But in the year 1774 three classic statements of the American interpretation of the imperial constitution appeared: James Wilson's *Considerations on the Nature and Extent of the Legislative Authority of the British Parliament*, Thomas Jefferson's *Summary View of the Rights of British America*, and John Adams' *Novanglus: or A History of the Dispute with America*. The first of these erudite justifications of the American legal argument is, in many respects, the most interesting of the three. Wilson declared that he had written it as early as 1770, a fact which, if established, would place him in the forefront of those who, besides assuming a position, defended it systematically. But more to the point is the fact that Wilson was a newcomer to America, a native of Scotland, and a scholar who had studied at St. Andrew's, Glasgow, and Edinburgh.

[2] *Commentaries* (Philadelphia, 1772), IV. 48, 49, 50, 51.
[3] Smyth, ed., *Writings of Benjamin Franklin*, V. 115.

[10]

Though Wilson, Jefferson and Adams approached the problem from different points of view, they arrived at substantially the same conclusions: that the colonies were not bound to respect the legislative supremacy of Parliament and that the constitutional structure of the empire was held together by the Crown and not by the sovereignty of Parliament. This theory of the imperial organization, so unacceptable to the ministers of George III and so prophetic of what the British Empire would one day become, was never more explicitly stated than by James Madison:

The fundamental principle of the Revolution was, that the Colonies were coordinate members with each other and with Great Britain, of an empire united by a common executive sovereign, but not united by any common legislative sovereign. The legislative power was maintained to be as complete in each American Parliament, as in the British Parliament. And the royal prerogative was in force in each Colony by virtue of its acknowledging the King for its executive magistrate, as it was in Great Britain by virtue of a like acknowledgment there. A denial of these principles by Great Britain, and the assertion of them by America, produced the Revolution.[4]

This issue, then, was no less than the enduring question of what an eighteenth-century pamphleteer called "the limits of sovereignty and the nature of civil subjection."[5] Those who defended the position of Blackstone and Mansfield could appeal to the constitutional bases of Parliament itself for their arguments. But the defenders of the American point of view were forced to appeal, at last, to the higher law of nature which governed all men and was supreme even over sovereign parliaments. Such was the ultimate resort of the ablest of the American writers, and their appeal to natural law received its formal expression in the Declaration of Independence.

[4] Gaillard Hunt, ed., *Writings of James Madison*, VI. 373.
[5] *Reflections on the Present State of the American War* (London, 1776), 2.

[11]

Such an appeal, resting upon an assumption of the sovereignty of the individual and carrying with it the corollary assumption of the inherent right of revolution, was justified by James Wilson in his first lectures as Professor of Law at the University of Pennsylvania in 1789. Fully aware of what he was about, Wilson set over against the Blackstonian theory of law what he hoped would become the *apologia* of the American Revolution and the foundation of an American system of jurisprudence unfettered by a narrow legalism.[6]

The issue was solved in the eighteenth century, as it was in America in the nineteenth, by the ultimate sanction of armed force—and both tests of "the limits of sovereignty and the nature of civil subjection" reached a *de facto* conclusion in the Commonwealth of Virginia, at Yorktown and at Appomattox. Since the issue seems to rest at bottom upon such a sanction, it is fruitless to debate the legal validity of the positions of Blackstone and Wilson, though this has been ably if inconclusively done by such modern scholars as McIlwain and Schuyler.[7] The final answer to such a problem may be that phrased by the Marquis de Chastellux in "a particular conversation with Mr. Samuel Adams." "I am clearly of opinion," he said, "that the Parliament of England had no right to tax America without her consent, but I am more clearly convinced that when a whole people say *we will be free,* it is difficult to demonstrate they are in the wrong."[8]

What is of far more importance is the fact that the con-

6 *D.A.B.,* XX. 329.

7 Charles H. McIlwain, *The American Revolution: A Constitutional Interpretation* (1923), and Robert L. Schuyler, *Parliament and the British Empire* (1929). Professor McIlwain challenged the generally accepted opinion of historians that the English argument, in a technical and legal sense, was the correct one, basing his arguments on precedents drawn from the relations of the realm and dominions and denying the validity of the American appeal to natural law. Professor Schuyler took the opposing view; cf. C. F. Mullett, *Fundamental Law and the American Revolution, 1760-1776* (1933), 161n., and R. G. Adams, *Political Ideas of the American Revolution* (1923). I am inclined to agree with the point of view defended by Professor Schuyler.

8 *Travels in America,* I. 217.

cepts of government and the nature of society that were emerging became embodied in the American structure of law: that, under the sovereignty of the individual, governments were limited in power; that acts of a government contrary to substantive law were void. Back of these concepts lay a considerable body of colonial experience in the problem of federalism, and if Franklin in 1768 found it difficult to accept a "middle ·doctrine" on this historic problem, he was not merely expressing its essential perplexity, but also its continuity. This "supreme problem of politics" had its background in the Confederation of the United Colonies of New England of 1643; in William Penn's proposed union of the colonies in 1697; in Daniel Coxe's Plan of Union of 1721; in the proposals of George Clinton, Thomas Penn, Governor Dinwiddie, and Richard Peters between 1744 and 1752; in the more famous plan presented by Benjamin Franklin at the Albany Congress of 1754. And it had its future in Alexander Hamilton's suggestion in 1780 for "a solid coercive union" and in James Madison's statement that

An individual independence of the States, is utterly irreconcilable with the idea of an aggregate sovereignty. I think, at the same time, that a consolidation of the States into one simple republic is not less unattainable than it would be inexpedient. Let it be tried, then, whether any middle ground can be taken, which will at once support a due supremacy of the national authority and leave in force the local authorities so far as they can be subordinately useful.[9]

Out of this colonial background of federalism, and in answer to the failure of the British ministry to find a workable distribution of authority between the whole and the separate parts, came the Articles of Confederation of 1781 and the Federal Constitution of 1787. Benjamin Franklin was one of the leading members of that notable Convention which wrote the elusive "middle doctrine" into American substantive law.

But if Franklin's Albany Plan of Union is a part of the

[9] Hunt, ed., *Writings*, II. 337-39.

[13]

continuity of experience that resulted in such a great contribution to the theory and practice of government, so are the similar efforts of Joseph Galloway. They failed of acceptance in America and in England, but so did the Albany Plan of 1754 fail. As the ideas of an American and a British subject who ably and conscientiously sought the middle doctrine, Galloway's various Plans of Union belong both to the history of American federalism and to the history of British imperialism. Their obscurity is due not so much to their failure as to the fact that they failed during the white heat of civil war, with all of its uncompromising hates and passions.

CHAPTER II

BACKGROUND OF A TORY

THERE IS no middle ground in revolution, but there are always those who seek it, only to discover its exposed dangers and its fruitlessness. Those who revolt in vindication of their rights or in assertion of their freedom and those who deny the right and the act of rebellion have only one foe—the enemy of their ideas. The ideas of the radical in revolt and the ideas of the conservative in suppression of revolt may have, even in their extreme form, some truth as well as some error. But those who endeavor to find a judicious balance between them, exposing their errors and composing their differences, usually win the enmity of both and seldom the gratitude of either. For in such crises, as Benjamin Franklin observed, "Passion governs, and she never governs wisely."

Joseph Galloway was one who took the dangerous and costly middle road in one of the most fateful moments of modern history. The story of the organic laws that he proposed, to accommodate the differences of those who denied the supremacy of Parliament and of those who supported it, is significant not merely as a story of futility and failure. It is significant also as affording some light on the sort of intellect that, in time of crisis, makes a stubborn choice of failure by clinging to the middle course. As such, it may be regarded as a footnote to the intellectual history of the American Revolution and as slightly more than a footnote to the perennial processes of the Tory mind. The historian may well ask himself what are the determining causes of such an intellectual approach to the ever present pressure of social forces against any inadequacies of political institutions.

Was it because Galloway was trained in the law, with a lawyer's respect for precedent and for the principles of the

British constitution, that he upheld the absolute supremacy of Parliament? There were other colonial lawyers who denied it: James Wilson, Thomas Jefferson, James Iredell, George Mason, John Adams, and others. Was it because he was wealthy and with widespread interests at stake that he abhorred revolutionary tendencies? Charles Carroll, George Washington, Robert Morris, and Philip Schuyler are some of the familiar names that come to mind. Was it because the Philadelphia social structure in which Galloway was firmly fixed exerted its subtle but powerful pressures? John Cadwalader, Joseph Reed, Richard Peters, and others were also Philadelphians of secure social position. Was it because he distrusted the people and was hostile to the leveling effects of republicanism? He himself, with the support of the so-called popular party, had dominated the Pennsylvania Assembly for a decade and had fought steadily against the proprietary government and the compact little circle around the Penns' governors. Was it because he sought favor and position in a British-controlled society with its graduated system of social rewards? He had thought seriously in 1773 and 1774 of retiring to the quiet "Trevose," his country seat in Bucks County. Was it because, in his professional and social life, he was insulated against the liberal ideas of the Age of Reason? He had been protégé and colleague of Benjamin Franklin for nearly a quarter of a century. His repudiation of Franklin's influence, and even of Franklin's deeply concerned solicitation, is the most puzzling question of all.

But evidence by contrast or analogy may be misleading. When Galloway's total heritage and total environment are taken into account, it may appear that all of these factors determined his course. It may be that the lawyer's respect for precedent, the wealthy man's concern for the protection of property, the aristocrat's concept of the place and value of gentility in society, the cultivated person's dislike of radicalism or violence, the responsible subject's concern for the future of the British empire—all these influences may have operated upon him. Political antipathies and personal dislikes —such as his long-standing rivalry with John Dickinson— undoubtedly had their influence. Even smaller and more indeterminate factors may have swayed his loyalties. One of his most intemperate pamphlets, written in the critical winter of 1774-75 when there was still an opportunity for conciliatory leaders to carry the day, was produced hastily while he was racked with fever. If he had been well, that pamphlet, which ended his influence in American affairs, might have been less inflammatory.

Galloway's background was that of a substantial, middle-class family of landowners, traders, and local officials.[1] The family seat, "Tulip Hill," where he was born about 1731, had been granted by Lord Baltimore to Richard Galloway in 1662 and was located in Anne Arundel County. The ships owned by one of his uncles, Samuel Galloway, traded with England and the West Indies. Two cousins married into the Shippen and Pemberton families of Pennsylvania. These family and business connections doubtless influenced his removal to Philadelphia after the death of his father. He took up the study of the law and about the age of eighteen was admitted to practice before the Supreme Court of the province. A year earlier he had received Philadelphia's social approval through admission to that most exclusive club, the Schuylkill Fishing Company, and in due time he gained further social recognition by membership in the Philadelphia Assembly. In 1753 he married Grace Growden, daughter of one of the wealthiest men in the province, former Speaker of the Assembly, justice of the Supreme Court, and Provincial Coun-

[1] A biography of Galloway is very much to be desired. Aside from a typed dissertation by Raymond C. Werner, "Joseph Galloway; His Life and Times" (University of Iowa, 1927), and the sketch in the *Dictionary of American Biography*, the most useful account is E. H. Baldwin's "Joseph Galloway: the Loyalist Politician," in the *Penn. Mag. of Hist. and Biog.*, XXVI. (1902) 161-91, 289-321, 417-42. The rather pathetic but revealing diary of Grace Growden Galloway is published, *ibid.*, LV. (1931) 32-94.

[17]

cilor. Growden was an owner of the famous Durham iron furnace and one of the few men in the province who could boast a four-wheeled coach. Galloway had come from a Quaker family, but his marriage to Grace Growden took place in Christ Church, an event which apparently caused him to lose his status in the Society of Friends, though Richard Peters described him in 1756 as "a young rising Quaker lawyer." There was no doubt that he was rising socially and professionally: the Schuylkill Fishing Company, the Philadelphia Assembly, Christ Church, marriage to a rich heiress—the familiar guarantees of prominence, if not success, were all his. In 1756 he was elected to the Pennsylvania Assembly.

Despite the fact that he had married into the circle of Proprietary officialdom, Galloway promptly allied himself with the anti-Proprietary or popular party led by Benjamin Franklin. This, no doubt, was due less to his independent political principles than to his dependence upon the support of the smoothly functioning political activities of the Society of Friends. At any rate he joined with Franklin in the attempt to tax the Proprietors' estates and to secure royal government for the province. This was the beginning of Galloway's interest in the theory of colonial government and the beginning as well of his political rivalry with John Dickinson. Dickinson also had been born in Maryland, in 1732, had studied law at the Inns of Court, had married the daughter of a former Speaker of the Assembly, and had thereby acquired one of the large provincial fortunes. Their backgrounds, so strikingly parallel, afford little explanation for their divergent approach to provincial problems. Both were of a legalistic bent of mind, both were conservative, both were enemies of radicalism and violence, yet for almost two decades they were bitterly divided on the issues that led to the Revolution. It was with fine impartiality that the College of New Jersey, at its commencement in 1769, gave to John Dickinson and to

Joseph Galloway the honorary degree of Doctor of Laws.[2] But this made Galloway no less suspicious of the republican tendencies of such leaders among the Presbyterians as Dr. John Witherspoon of Princeton, as one of his Plans of Union later indicated.

As a leader in the Pennsylvania Assembly, and its powerful Speaker from 1765 to 1774, Galloway more than once "remarkably displayed his talents of eloquence and an extensive knowledge of the laws of England and the judicial processes used in our mother country."[3] But, championing the rights of the Assembly, he sacrificed broader imperial interests for the sake of increasing the power of the legislature and of embarrassing the Proprietary government. Even before the drafting of Franklin's Albany Plan of 1754, Thomas Penn had urged intercolonial union for defense against France, and the popular party in the Assembly had ignored or nullified his proposals by injecting the question of taxing the Proprietors' estates into the problem of frontier defense. As an Indian Commissioner from the Assembly at the Indian Treaty at Easton in 1757, Galloway seriously interfered with the imperial control of Indian affairs by lending his office to the extra-legal activities of the Friendly Association formed by members of the Society of Friends.[4] "The colonies," Galloway later wrote for an English audience, "had amply demonstrated to the home government that no form of united action, political, economic, or military was at that time possible . . . and that any unity which might be brought about to enable them to maintain their new western frontiers by their own efforts must be formed from without."[5] Thomas Penn would have been gratified if Galloway had supported such views as a leader of the Assembly.

[2] This honor, it has been suggested, may have come about through the influence of Governor William Franklin, a warm friend of Galloway and a member, ex-officio, of the board of trustees of the college.

[3] "Journal of Samuel Foulke," Penn. Mag. of Hist. and Biog., VIII. 409.

[4] J. P. Boyd, "Indian Affairs in Pennsylvania, 1737-1760," in Indian Treaties Printed by Benjamin Franklin (Philadelphia, 1938).

[5] [Galloway], Historical and Political Reflections (London, 1780), 7-11.

[19]

In the proceedings of the Assembly against Justice William Moore and Dr. William Smith for publishing an alleged libel against the legislature, Galloway gave the support of his leadership to a suspension of writs of habeas corpus and to legislative moves against the freedom of the press. When, in 1764, the Assembly's exhaustive bickering with the Proprietary party and indifference to frontier defense led to demands from Scots-Irish Presbyterians for more equal representation of the populous western counties in the legislature, Galloway stood out against what he thought to be dangerous republicanism. Despite all of Galloway's legislative activity that helped to make intercolonial union impossible, he could declare that

There is no alternative between this measure [a military establishment in the Colonies] and a general union to ensure us protection against the foreign invader. Such an union [that of the Albany Congress of 1754] has been already rejected and such an one we shall now never enjoy. Our superiors think it convenient to keep us in another state; and therefore we shall undoubtedly have this measure . . . established whether the government is changed or not.[6]

The debate was carried to the electorate in one of the bitterest campaigns in colonial history, and both Galloway and Franklin were defeated. "Mr. Franklin died like a philosopher," wrote a contemporary, "But Mr. Galloway *agonized in Death*, like a Mortal Deist, who has no Hopes of a Future Existence."[7] The defeat was temporary, for he was returned again in 1765.

But Galloway's resurrection only brought him into office again at a time when the broad issues of colonial reorganization made it impossible for him, despite his identification with a so-called popular party, to conceal his inherent conservatism and his distrust of popular movements. There appears to be no contemporary evidence that he favored the

[6] Baldwin, *op. cit.*, XXVI. 183.
[7] W. B. Reed, *Life of Joseph Reed*, I. 36.

Stamp Act, though he was immediately charged with it, but he was alarmed at the evidence of lawless and riotous behavior that the Act had produced in the colonies. Over the signature of "Americanus" in the *Pennsylvania Journal* for January 9, 1766, he warned his countrymen against measures that had the color of sedition and declared that, unless such activities ceased, Parliament would be forced to use its power to suppress them. This first evidence of Galloway's loyalist inclinations caused widespread indignation and, according to the later testimony of William Franklin, brought upon him the stigma of being called a Tory. The lawless opposition to the Stamp Act, or at least much of the responsibility for it, Galloway attributed to the republicanism of the Presbyterians. "A certain sect of people," he wrote Franklin, "if I may judge from all their late conduct, seem to look on this as a favorable opportunity of establishing their republican principles and of throwing off all connection with their mother country."[8] He further revealed his true sentiments in the address of the Assembly to the Crown—which he wrote in appreciation of the repeal of the Stamp Act—a part of which bears striking resemblance to expressions that he later used in support of his Plans of Union:

Fully sensible how much the happiness of your people depends on a perfect harmony and connection between Great Britain and her colonies, we assure your Majesty that no care or endeavours shall be wanting, on our part, to promote and establish that union of affections and interest so essential to the welfare of both, and to preserve that loyalty and affection to your Majesty's person and government which we esteem to be one of their first and most important duties.[9]

In the ensuing election of 1766 the Presbyterian party issued a broadside entitled *Six Arguments again Chusing Joseph Galloway an Assemblyman*, the first argument being that he had charged with disloyalty those who had sought to

[8] Baldwin, *op. cit.*, XXVI. 292.
[9] *Ibid.*, 293.

[21]

preserve American rights and that he had long deceived the people by his "pretended zeal for liberty."[10] Again he was elected, but popular opinion in the colonies was swiftly moving ahead of him.

Almost as soon as he had published his "Americanus" warning against seditious and lawless proceedings, he expanded the article into a pamphlet entitled *Political Reflections on the Dispute between Great Britain and her Colonies respecting her Right of Imposing Taxes on them without their Assent.* This pamphlet, which was never published, was concerned less with the theory of Parliamentary supremacy than with Galloway's belief that the Americans had been "so worked up as to be ready even for rebellion itself."[11] When Lord Hillsborough in 1768 called upon colonial governors to prorogue their assemblies if they proposed any action on the Massachusetts Circular Letter affirming the unconstitutionality of Parliamentary taxation, Galloway, in his *Pacificus to the Public,* defended Hillsborough and attacked the "factious" and "turbulent" colony of Massachusetts. When John Dickinson's *Letters of a Pennsylvania Farmer* swept through the colonies with their ringing statement of American rights, Galloway, finding his old enemy warning Americans "to be on their guard against men who set examples of servility" by such phrases as filled the address of the Assembly to the Crown, separated himself even farther from the feelings of his countrymen.

This he did by his injudicious remarks to William Goddard, whom he had helped establish the *Pennsylvania Chronicle* as an anti-Proprietary paper and with whom he had split when that unhappy partnership foundered. While Goddard was not an unprejudiced witness, there were many Pennsylvanians who accepted without question what he had to say about Galloway's comment on the *Pennsylvania Farmer:*

[10] *Ibid.,* 294-95.
[11] Galloway to Franklin, Jan. 13, 1766; Werner, *op. cit.,* 111; Sparks, *Writings of Franklin,* VII, 303-305.

Mr. *Galloway* exclaimed, with a countenance expressive of the deepest envy, that they were "damned ridiculous! mere stuff! fustian! altogether stupid, inconsistent! Only a compilation by *Dickinson* and *Thomson!*" . . . Mr. *Galloway* ridiculed my notions about liberty and the rights of mankind, and he observed that "the people in *America* were mad—they knew not what they wanted—and indeed were incapable of judging on such matters— that such factious pieces would answer for the selectmen of *Boston*, and the mob meetings of *Rhode Island*, but he was sure that they would soon be despised here, *Pennsylvanians* (a few hot-headed people excepted) being of a different make, of more solidity, none of *your* damned republican breed—but loyal to the king and friends to monarchy."[12]

Whether Galloway was correctly quoted or not, there were many people in America ready to accept the word of a colonial editor who believed in liberty and the rights of mankind.

The persistent attacks upon Galloway in the newspapers and in pamphlets caused him to think of retiring from public life, but Franklin wrote frequent and affectionate letters from London urging him not "to bury in private retirement so early, all the usefulness of so much experience and great abilities."[13] Franklin, three thousand miles away from the turmoil of provincial politics, could scarcely appreciate the extent to which his old colleague had alienated himself from the sentiments of a large section of the public.[14] The years of experience gained in dominating the Assembly, the exhausting and unsuccessful struggle to overthrow the Proprietary government, the bitter feud with the ascendant star of the *Pennsylvania Farmer*, to say nothing of such annoying epi-

[12] William Goddard, *The Partnership: or The History of the Rise and Progress of the Pennsylvania Chronicle,* &c. (Philadelphia, 1770), 16-18; See also, A. M. Schlesinger, "The Press and Politics," *Penn. Mag. of Hist. and Biog.,* LX. 309-22. Benjamin Franklin wrote on Jan. 30, 1772: "I cast my eye over Goddard's Piece against our friend Mr. Galloway, and then lit my fire with it"; Smyth, *Writings of Franklin,* V. 378.

[13] *Penn. Mag. of Hist. and Biog.,* XXVI. 302.

[14] So savage was Goddard's attack that Galloway, fearing defeat in the election of 1770, stood for the assembly that year in Bucks County rather than, as before, in Philadelphia, *ibid.,* LX. 320.

[23]

sodes as the incident with Goddard, had resulted chiefly in disillusionment and a growing distrust of the ability of the people to govern themselves. After 1770 Galloway's public utterances and activities contrasted strikingly with his earlier career: he was deeply concerned now with larger problems than the narrow provincial interests that had occupied his attention in his first years in the Assembly. He felt, as he wrote Richard Jackson early in 1774, that the Stamp Act controversy had done much harm both in England and in America: both sides had taken extreme positions and both sides should make concessions in a conciliatory move for the sake of the empire.

In his speech in the Assembly on the resolution to petition for a royal government, Galloway had implied that he felt the Albany Plan of Union was desirable and should have been adopted. He was familiar with that Plan and had doubtless read the pamphlets of Archibald Kennedy and had talked with Franklin about it. Fearful of what the unchecked opposition of Massachusetts radicals might lead to, and being genuinely loyal to the British form of government, Galloway now turned his thoughts—as the public press and all thoughtful Americans were doing—to the larger problem of the imperial relation. Franklin, even in the 1760's, had come to believe that Parliament had no right to legislate for the colonies —even for the province of Pennsylvania, whose charter expressly reserved to Parliament the right to levy duties. As for "the Principle that by settling under that Charter we contracted to submit to such Duties," Franklin wrote to Galloway in 1769, "I am not myself of that Opinion, but have never been able to reason any other Person out of it."[15] He was in advance of most of his contemporaries in thinking of the empire as made up of "different states," subject to the same Crown, and in regarding Parliament as having "Power only *within the Realm.*" When the author of *An Inquiry into the Nature and Causes of the Present Disputes* wrote in 1769

[15] Franklin to Galloway, Jan. 9, 1769; MS in William L. Clements Library.

[24]

that "Our right of legislation over the Americans . . . is asserted by most, doubted by some, and wholly disclaimed by a few," Franklin wrote in the margin of his copy: "I am one of those few, but am persuaded the time is not far distant, when the few will become the many; for *Magna est Veritas, et praevalebit*."[16]

Galloway received from Franklin in 1769 one of the briefest and most alliterative plans of conciliation on record: "Of late," Franklin wrote,

a Cry begins to arise, Can no body propose a Plan of Conciliation? Must we ruin ourselves by intestine Quarrels? I was ask'd in Company lately by a noble Lord if I had no Plan of that kind to propose? My answer was, 'Tis easy to propose a Plan; mine may be express'd in a few Words; *Repeal* the Laws, *Renounce* the Right, *Recall* the Troops, *Refund* the Money, and *Return to the old Method of Requisition*. I have no Objection, says he, to repealing the Laws and recalling the Soldiers; and as to refunding the Money, I believe it may be easily done; for I suppose what we have receiv'd amounts to no great matter. But why would you insist on our Renouncing the Right? How can you expect it when you see your own little Assemblies think themselves above *rescinding*? I do not insist upon that, says I; if continuing the Claim pleases you, continue it as long as you please, provided you never attempt to execute it. We shall consider it in the same Light with the Claim of the Spanish Monarch to the Title of King of Jerusalem.[17]

Galloway was too much of a legalist to follow his wise preceptor in such reasoning.

Plans of conciliation and plans of union were, however, being advanced in England and in America. Though Governor Bernard had written in 1765 that there was a general realization in the colonies that representation in Parliament would weaken their claim for exclusive jurisdiction in internal affairs, "Amor Patriae" published in December 1770 *A*

[16] Verner Crane, *Benjamin Franklin, Englishman and American* (1936), 117, 124, 125, 127.

[17] Franklin to Galloway, Jan. 9, 1769; MS in William L. Clements Library.

[25]

Plan of Union by admitting Representatives from the American Colonies, and from Ireland into the British Parliament.[18] The author of this Plan of Union is unknown, but Galloway himself indicated privately in 1774 that he thought American representation in Parliament was preferable to other plans. "Amor Patriae's" Plan of Union provided for fifty colonial representatives from thirty British provinces to the House of Commons and for ten "Lords for the principal Provinces and Islands, as soon as found convenient to be created by the royal Prerogative." This provision, too, was one that Galloway later looked upon with approval. The colonial representatives were to be elected by the provincial legislatures and were to be allowed "perhaps six months" for writs of election because of the distance. Moreover, the author argued,

. . . it would be wise and conciliating to enact in the proposed Act, granting the Honour of Representation, that neither America nor Ireland, shall be afterwards liable to be taxed separately or apart from the British, towards raising a Revenue, or for general Protection and Defence: This it is humbly conceived would be much wiser than to fix any limited Sums, on Account of the probable growing Population and Abilities af America in future; and although it might appear an Indignity to the supreme legislative Power to be limited by her own Subjects, it nevertheless would be a Manifestation of Wisdom, Justice and Prudence, for the said Supreme Power, so to limit their own Operations for the Peace, Safety and Satisfaction of the Publick.

If "Amor Patriae" was an American, his deferential acknowledgment of Parliamentary supremacy over the whole empire placed him, even in 1770, far to the rear of American imperial thinking. By 1774, when Wilson, Adams, and Jefferson came forth with their brilliant arguments asserting a status of colonial equality within the empire, even John Dickinson had moved up to the point at which he could attempt

[18] Broadside in the Historical Society of Pennsylvania. There is nothing in the broadside to show whether it was printed in America or in England.

to draw the line between what Parliament could and could not do with respect to the colonies.

Though events at the eve of the meeting of the Continental Congress had passed beyond Galloway, he was still the most powerful political figure in the province. He was still strong enough to keep Dickinson out of the first delegation to the Congress. But that strength was itself a weakness. Control of the Pennsylvania Assembly was control, for the most part, over men of little ability. That legislative body, wrote a contemporary,

made but a scurvy appearance . . . it was enough to make one sweat to see a parcel of countrymen sitting with their hats on, great coarse cloth coats, leather breeches, and woolen stockings in the month of July. There was not a speech made the whole time; whether their silence proceeded from their modesty or from their ability to speak, I know not.[19]

Political manipulation of an assembly of unlettered farmers and justices of the peace was one thing. But association in a Congress of some of the best minds in America—including a John Adams, a Roger Sherman, a John Jay, a Richard Henry Lee, an Edward Rutledge—was quite a different matter. Galloway, perhaps made proud and arrogant by his power over the Assembly and certainly made distrustful of the abilities of the common people, prepared for the Congress in the summer of 1774, fearful of its purpose and convinced of its illegality. His fears were not allayed by the knowledge that Sam Adams was to be among the delegates.

[19] Baldwin, *op. cit.*, XXVI. 296.

CHAPTER III

CIVIL GOVERNMENT OR CIVIL WAR?

THOSE WHO CHOOSE the path of mediation often insulate themselves from potential allies and ready information by the forbidding outward aspects of conservatism. Probably because he wore an "air of reserve, design, and cunning"— or so John Adams thought—Galloway knew less about what was transpiring in his native Philadelphia on Saturday evening, September 3, 1774, than he would have known if he had had the open conviviality of a Lee or a Harrison. That day, amid the quiet of Trevose, Galloway wrote to William Franklin, Governor of New Jersey. He had been to Philadelphia, had dined with some of the delegates to the Continental Congress and had observed the conduct of others. The Boston representatives, he thought, were "warm" and wished for a non-importation agreement, but were "in their Behaviour and Conversation very modest, and yet . . . not so much so as not to throw out Hints, which, like Straws and Feathers, tell us from which Point of the Compass the Wind comes." Nevertheless, Galloway thought the delegates generally would "behave with Temper and Moderation."[1]

On that same day, perhaps as Galloway wrote, there was a meeting at Thomas Mifflin's that would have shown him even more disconcertingly which direction the wind was taking. Mifflin's hospitality brought forth plain statements rather than sly hints. Among his guests were Dr. John Witherspoon of the College of New Jersey, who had entered "with great spirit into the American cause . . . [and was] an animated Son of Liberty"; Richard Henry Lee of Virginia, who had

[1] Edmund C. Burnett, *Letters of Members of the Continental Congress,* I. 5.

[28]

drunk Burgundy with John Dickinson all afternoon and who was "absolutely certain" that the same ship which carried to England a non-importation resolution would bring back a repeal of all the Coercive Acts; Benjamin Harrison, also of Virginia, who had "said he would have come on foot rather than not come"; Edward Rutledge of South Carolina who had affected fright at the mention of the name of George III and had said that "his promises are not worth anything." There were toasts aplenty at Mifflin's: Benjamin Harrison proposed "A constitutional death to the Lords Bute, Mansfield, and North," and Robert Treat Paine offered: "May the Collision of British flint and American steel produce that spark of liberty which shall illumine the latest posterity." There were other toasts, guardedly expressed, but meaningful enough as eyes met over glasses: "May the result of the Congress answer the expectations of the people." There were, to be sure, others that would have pleased Galloway: "Union of the Colonies" and "Union of Britain and the Colonies on a constitutional foundation."[2] But Mifflin, the most radical member of Pennsylvania's delegation, was host that September evening to men from Massachusetts and from Virginia, and their determined ideas about American rights and Parliamentary jurisdiction produced a union of sentiment that spelled triumph for America but doom for those who sought to remedy the imperial constitution by persuasive logic.

The opening session of the Congress two days later revealed to Galloway what he might have learned at Mifflin's. The first blow to his influence came over the choice of a meeting place. The City had offered Carpenter's Hall; Galloway, as Speaker of the Assembly, offered the State House. The latter was obviously the better place, "but," as Silas Deane put it, "as *he* offers [it], the other party oppose."[3] That was hard enough, but scarcely had the Congress come to

[2] *Ibid.*, I. 3-4.
[3] To Mrs. Deane, Sept. 5-6, 1774; Conn. Hist. Soc., *Collections*, II. 172; Burnett, *op. cit.*, I. 11.

order in Carpenter's Hall before the blow was repeated. Charles Thomson, whom John Adams had paid the tribute of calling "the Sam Adams of Philadelphia, the life of the cause of liberty,"[4] who had been Galloway's implacable foe in provincial politics, and whom Galloway had kept out of the Pennsylvania delegation, was chosen Secretary of the Congress. "This proceeding," wrote Silas Deane, "is highly agreeable to the mechanics and citizens in general, but mortifying in the last degree to Mr. Galloway and his party, Thomson being his sworn opposite, as you may say."[5] Galloway, smothering his surprise, did not think it prudent to oppose Thomson's nomination and he was elected unanimously. But the letter that Galloway wrote to Governor Franklin that evening was far less optimistic than the one he had written on Saturday:

I cannot say but from this Day's Appearance and Proceedings, I have altered very much my last Sentiments. The Virginians and Carolinians, Rutlidge excepted, seem much among the Bostonians, and have at their instance adopted the two above Measures. The Gentlemen from New York have as little Expectations of much Satisfaction from the Event of Things as myself.[6]

It was apparent that there was a rough geographical cleavage in the Congress: New England and Southern zealots against Middle States moderates. But Galloway had another stratification for the opinions of men on this great issue, the stratification of the conservative who saw cherished institutions threatened by violent and revolutionary forces. "One party [in the Congress]," he wrote some years later,

intended candidly and clearly to define American rights, and explicitly and dutifully to petition for the remedy which would redress the grievances justly complained of—to form a more solid and constitutional union between the two countries, and to avoid every measure which tended to sedition, or acts of violent opposi-

[4] *Ibid.*, I. 1.
[5] *Ibid.*, I. 11.
[6] *N. J. Archives*, 1st. ser., X. 477; Burnett, *op. cit.*, I. 9-10.

tion. The other consisted of persons, whose design, from the beginning of their opposition to the Stamp Act, was to throw off all subordination and connexion with Great-Britain; who meant by every fiction, falsehood and fraud, to delude the people from their due allegiance, to throw the subsisting Governments into anarchy, to incite the ignorant and vulgar to arms, and with those arms to establish American Independence. The one were men of loyal principles, and possessed of the Greatest fortunes in America; the other were Congregational and Presbyterian republicans, or men of bankrupt fortunes, overwhelmed in debt to the British merchants.[7]

It is not enough to say that Galloway was blind in stamping such men as John Adams, Richard Henry Lee, Roger Sherman, George Washington, George Read, Peyton Randolph, and Thomas Lynch with charges of falsehood, republicanism, bankruptcy, and debt. Lord North, George III, and British officialdom generally shared that opinion.[8] But it is important that Galloway believed the Americans were misled and misguided by a few dominant radicals, self-seekers, and demagogues. He believed it so firmly that, unlike such moderates as Jay, Duane, Dickinson, and the elder Rutledge, he prepared himself for defeat by clinging to a delusion as great as that he imagined the American people to be under. Shocked by the relatively trivial events of the first day in Congress, he reacted with the true conservative's self-defeating reserve in the face of hostile forces. He consorted with others who shared his views, drawing from them both comfort and exaggeration of his opinions, and he avoided those who differed with him. Assemblies of men are not only not won by such methods, but—particularly such an astute body as the first Continental Congress—are quick to discern the difference between that judicious restraint which evidences a mind open to conviction and that discreet behavior in the face of a hostile majority which conceals a mind already made up.

[7] *Historical and Political Reflections*, 66.
[8] E.g., Sir John Fortescue, ed., *Correspondence of King George the Third*, III, Introduction.

There was no doubt in which category Galloway stood. He stood in 1774, wrote John Adams, just where the Hutchinsonian faction were in 1764—that is, concealing his real convictions with respect to American rights by "Machiavellian dissimulation."[9] But the fact is that Galloway did not share his thoughts and feelings with John Adams or Richard Henry Lee as he did with John Jay and James Duane. Toward the end of the Congress this attitude of Galloway and other conservatives bore fruit in Patrick Henry's embittered comment: "Their System . . ." Henry had said, "would ruin the cause of America." And he was very impatient in beholding such men "and not to be at liberty to describe them in their true colors."[10] Galloway, nevertheless, came very close to securing the adoption of his Plan of Union by the Congress. That he did not succeed is the one great negative fact of that notable assembly, and it is perhaps not too much to say that he was the chief instrument in bringing about his own defeat.

The thoroughness of his preparations for the Congress only added to the general appearance of dissimulation. During the preceding summer he had laid the foundations for his policy of constitutional accommodation. He had drafted the communication of the Pennsylvania Committee of Correspondence addressed to the Massachusetts Committee, and in it he had insisted that the defense of American rights should be left to the duly constituted representatives of the people in their colonial legislatures; that every act of violence or even the appearance of it should be carefully avoided; that the first step should be a congress of delegates chosen by the legislatures of the colonies; and that it might be expected such a congress, constitutionally chosen, would "establish a political union between the two countries with the assent of both, which would effectually secure to Americans their

9 C. F. Adams, ed., *Works of John Adams*, II. 361-62.
10 *Ibid.*, II. 396.

future rights and privileges."[11] Having chosen this course, Galloway caused the Pennsylvania legislature to instruct its delegates to the Continental Congress to use their "utmost endeavors to form and adopt a plan which shall afford the best prospect of obtaining a redress of American grievances, ascertaining American rights and establishing that union and harmony which is most essential to the welfare and happiness of both countries."[12] With such a legal mandate, he set about the drafting of his own Plan of Union.

To prepare the minds of the people for such a program, he wrote a pamphlet entitled *Arguments on Both Sides in the Dispute between Great-Britain and her Colonies. In which those in Favor of the Power of Parliament to bind the Colonies are stated and answered, and the Rights of the Colonists explained and asserted on new and just Principles. By a Sincere Friend to both Countries.*[13] This pamphlet is interesting not for the novelty of its arguments—they were not only familiar arguments, but were later restated in much the same form in Galloway's more famous *Candid Examination*—but for its restrained impartiality and for its subsequent fate. The pamphlet was printed on the eve of the Congress, but Galloway, uncertain what the temper of the delegates would be, withheld publication. He transmitted a copy to Governor Franklin, and Franklin immediately forwarded it to the Earl of Dartmouth, together with copies of two of Galloway's letters, marked "secret and confidential."[14] Galloway, secretly

[11] Peter Force, ed., *Am. Archives,* I. 486.

[12] *Pennsylvania Packet,* Sept. 5, 1774; *Examination of Joseph Galloway, Esq., by . . . the House of Commons,* ed. Thomas Balch (Philadelphia, 1855), 42-43.

[13] *N. J. Arch.,* 1st ser., X. 478-94.

[14] *Ibid.,* X. 473-78; on November 2 Dartmouth thanked Franklin for this information and promised that it would be "kept most secret and communicated only to the King's Confidential Servants"; *ibid.,* X. 501. On Feb. 25, 1775, Franklin wrote to Galloway: "Permit me to hint to you that it is whispered here by ministerial people that yourself and Mr. Jay of New York, are friends to their measures, and give them private intelligence of the views of the popular or country party in America. I do not believe this; but I thought it a duty of friendship to acquaint you with the report"; Bigelow, ed., *Works of Franklin,* V. 435-39.

communicating information to a royal governor for transmission to English officials, withheld from the Congress and the public the one product of his pen that lacked an obvious and aggravating animus.

Nevertheless he submitted his Plan of Union to Congress on September 28. There are two sets of the resolutions with which it was introduced, differing chiefly in that one called for an appeal from the Congress to the Crown and the other recommended the Plan of Union to the colonial legislatures.[15] The former appears to have been the version laid before Congress. But both agreed "that the Colonies hold in abhorrence the idea of being considered independent communities on the British government and most ardently desire the establishment of a Political Union, not only among themselves, but with the Mother State, upon those principles of safety and freedom which are essential in the Constitution of all free governments." Both agreed also that "the Colonies from their local circumstances, cannot be represented in the Parliament of Great-Britain." Galloway had evidently led William Franklin to believe that he would advocate colonial representation in Parliament. "The principal Part of his Plan is, as I am told," wrote Franklin to Dartmouth, "the making an Application for Leave *to send Representatives from each Colony in America to the Parliament in Great Britain*; a Measure which, notwithstanding the many Difficulties and Objections made thereto, on both Sides of the Water, he thinks will be the only effectual Remedy for the present Evils, and prove a lasting and beneficial Cement to all the Parts of the British Empire."[16] And just before the opening of the Congress Galloway had talked with the "elder Rutledge of South Carolina, whose sentiments and mine differ in no one particular, so far as I explained myself, and I was reserved in no point save that of a representation in Parliament."[17]

[15] W. C. Ford, ed., *Journals of the Continental Congress*, I. 43, 48-49.
[16] *N. J. Arch.*, 1st. ser., X. 474-75.
[17] *Ibid.*, X. 475.

Apparently Galloway's Plan of Union did not represent altogether what he desired, but rather what he hoped the delegates would accept.

The resolution was moved in a long speech by Galloway— of which there are also two versions: one in the form of John Adams' notes and the other expanded from Galloway's notes and printed in his *Historical and Political Reflections on the Rise and Progress of the American Rebellion.*[18] Since this pamphlet was published in London in 1780, it is to be expected that its version of the speech would differ somewhat from Adams' abbreviated notes. The former was published for the British public and for the eyes of a government bent on suppressing rebellion; the latter was addressed to a group of able men singularly conscious of their rights and possessed by a high determination to sustain them. The differences of the two versions are many and startling: according to Adams, Galloway said the Americans protested against the Stamp Act "with the greatest reason and justice." According to Galloway's own version, he said that "Parliament was naturally led to exercise the power which had been, by its predecessors, so often exercised over the Colonies, and to pass the Stamp Act. Against this act, the Colonies petitioned Parliament, and denied its authority. . . . This justly alarmed the British Senate. It was thought and called by the ablest men and Britain, a clear and explicit declaration of the American Independence, and compelled the Parliament to pass the Declaratory Act, in order to save its ancient and incontrovertible right of supremacy over all the parts of the empire."[19] Again, according to Adams: "I am as much a friend of liberty as exists; and no man shall go further in point of fortune, or in point of blood, than the man who now addresses you." And according to Galloway: "Desirous as I am to promote the freedom of the Colonies . . . I must intreat you to desert the Measures which have been so injudiciously and ineffectu-

[18] C. F. Adams, ed., *Works of John Adams,* II. 388.
[19] Ford, ed., *Journals,* I. 45*ff.*; *Hist. and Pol. Reflections,* 70.

ally pursued by antecedent assemblies." Galloway's version also speaks openly against the non-importation agreement and acknowledges his own conviction that representation in Parliament was "the most perfect union in power and liberty with the parent state," important matters on which the Adams' notes are silent. But Galloway must be permitted some latitude because of the five years in time, three thousand miles of space, and the unbridgeable chasm in the political views of his audiences that separated the two versions of his speech. If we accept the Adams version as being the substance of what he actually said, the speech was as well tempered and as conciliatory as the *Arguments on Both Sides* from which much of it was drawn.

The Plan of Union thus presented to Congress provided for an American legislature "for regulating the administration of the general affairs of America." Much as Galloway disliked the charter governments of New England or the proprietary governments, such as Pennsylvania, he nevertheless sacrificed his own convictions by providing that each colony was to retain its existing form of government and the power of regulating its own internal police. The general American legislature was to be composed of a president general, appointed by the king during pleasure, and a grand council, chosen triennially by the legislatures of the colonies. The grand council was to meet annually and to possess "all the like rights, liberties, and privileges as are held and exercised by and in the House of Commons of Great-Britain." The assent of the president general was required to validate acts of the council, and the president and council were to exercise all "rights, powers and authorities, necessary for regulating and administering all the general police and affairs of the colonies . . . as well civil and criminal as commercial." Galloway, however, could not concede his favorite doctrine of the supremacy of Parliament, and so he provided that the American legislature was to be "an *inferior* and distinct branch of the British legislature." The "great principle [of

[36]

the Plan] was," so Galloway wrote twenty years later, "that no law should bind America without her consent."[20] Thus he provided that legislative bills respecting America might be introduced either in the Parliament at Westminster or in the American legislature, but in order to become law all bills were required to have the assent of both bodies.

This was the first serious proposal of an Anglo-American organic law since the plan of the Albany Congress of 1754. Galloway had indeed studied the earlier plan and was doubtless influenced by it. He was accused, in fact, of drawing his ideas from that plan, but the reply to the accusation—perhaps written by Galloway himself—was that the plan of 1754 was a union for the colonies only, providing for an inferior legislature without any connection with the British Parliament.[21] Even with its central idea that no law should bind America without her consent, the Plan submitted by Galloway was not proposed as a "perfect plan," nor, as he told the House of Commons Committee on Papers in June 1779, "altogether as a plan of my judgment." He approved the plan as far as it went, but thought it would admit of "some very material additions." These additions were not included for fear the delegates to Congress would thereby be driven from "the ground of accommodation." He likewise told the Committee that "some of the best men [in the Congress] . . . espoused the plan."

In this he was correct. The New York delegation seconded his proposal. James Duane made the seconding speech, and John Jay supported him. Edward Rutledge of South Carolina thought that the Plan might be free from every objection, and added that he regarded it as "almost a perfect plan." But Richard Henry Lee believed it would so alter the Constitu-

[20] Galloway to Thomas McKean, March 7, 1793; McKean Papers, Hist. Soc. of Pa., II. 108.
[21] *Pa. Journal*, April 3, 1775; *Pa. Gazette*, April 26, 1775. The writer in the *Gazette* said that Galloway had carried the Albany Plan into Congress for purposes of comparison and in order to have improvements made; cf. Burnett, *op. cit.*, I. 51n.

tion of the colonial legislatures that he could not agree to it without consulting his constituents. Patrick Henry declared that it would "liberate our constituents from a corrupt House of Commons, but throw them into the arms of an American Legislature, that may be bribed by that nation which avows, in the face of the world, that bribery is a part of her system of government." Galloway, encouraged by the support of Rutledge, Jay, and Duane, made a second speech, but the motion was tabled and subsequently "rejected and ordered to be kept out of the minutes."[22]

The Congress adjourned on October 26. It had adopted everything that Galloway feared—a non-importation agreement, an approval of the Suffolk resolves, a justification of the rights of Americans as the "born heirs of freedom"—and it had rejected everything that he had hoped for. Nevertheless, he thought, and continued in the illusory hope for over a decade, that it was not yet too late. If his zealous compatriots would not listen, perhaps others would. The Plan was "much handed about at New York," William Franklin wrote to Dartmouth, "and greatly approved of by some of the most sensible Men of that City."[23] Galloway himself sent copies to Dr. Franklin in London, and Franklin showed them to Lord Chatham and Lord Camden. "They seem'd to think the Idea ingenious," wrote Franklin,

but the Mode so new as to require much attentive thought before a Judgment of it could be form'd. From something dropt by Lord Gower the other Day in the House of Lords, accusing the Congress sharply of rejecting a *Plan of Union* with Britain, after it had been recev'd, and ordering the Vote for receiving it to be erased out of their Minutes, I imagine the Ministry are in possession of it; if on Enquiry I find are not, I shall communicate it to them, as possibly it may bring on Some Negociation and stay their Hands from Blood, of which I grieve to say there is but little prospect. For everything is hurried with inconceivable Precipita-

[22] Burnett, *op. cit.*, I. 51, 53-54.
[23] *N. J. Arch.*, 1st. ser., X. 504.

tion & every thing rejected immediately, the Consideration of which might occasion Delay.[24]

As for himself, Franklin had written to Galloway a year earlier:

I wish most sincerely with you that a Constitution was formed and Settled for America, that we might know what we are and what we have, what our Rights and what our Duties, in the Judgment of this Country as well as our own. Till such a Constitution is settled, different Sentiments will ever occasion Misunderstandings. But if this is to be settled, it must settle itself, nobody here caring for the Trouble of thinking on't.[25]

Now that Galloway in America had produced a constitution, Franklin felt he could not "but apprehend more Mischief than Benefit from a closer Union. . . . It seems like Mezentius' coupling and binding together the dead and the living."[26] A quarter of a century earlier Franklin had caught the vision of America's future greatness; in 1754 he had sought to bind the colonies together in the interest of the British empire; and in 1760 he had declared "that the *foundations of the future grandeur and stability of the British empire lie in America*; and though, like other foundations, they are low and little seen, they are, nevertheless, broad and strong enough to support the greatest political structure human wisdom ever yet erected."[27] Now, however, he saw what his son and his close friend Galloway could not see: that the American empire must choose its own path of destiny. That they could not see it was a poignant and overwhelming disappointment to the aging diplomat. But his own course was clear and unswerving.

The disappointments and the fears induced by the Congress, mild as the determinations of that body may seem,

[24] Franklin to Galloway, Feb. 5, 1775; MS in William L. Clements Library.
[25] Same to same, Feb. 18, 1774; *ibid.*
[26] Bigelow, ed., *Works of Franklin*, V. 435-39.
[27] Smyth, ed., *Writings of Franklin*, IV. 4.

caused Galloway to do what could only aggravate his bitterness and widen the chasm between him and his country's cause. He went off to New York to talk with others who shared his feelings—the Duanes, the Verplancks, the Hoffmans, the De Lanceys. Hesitant doubt gave way to unalterable conviction as hostility to anything savoring of republicanism fed upon itself. Republicanism became synonymous in Galloway's mind with the aims of farmers, small merchants, artisans, debtors, paper-money agitators, and leveling Presbyterians. The protection of property being one of the primary concerns of government, government in turn should take its direction from property. Power or the assumption of power in the hands of the propertyless was therefore a subversion of government, a dangerous radicalism to be abhorred even more than the threat of parliamentary tyranny. "The men of Property," he wrote half wishfully to Samuel Verplanck, "begin to think & speak their Sentiments, and I hope will in a little time take that Lead which their Consequence entitle them to. But I conclude this will not be the case until the measures of Parliament are known, and they can hope to be protected in their upright conduct." This comes close to uncloaking Galloway's real convictions on government: the Rights of Man become the Rights of Property. In the next breath he added: "A Committee has been appointed for this [Bucks] County by a few warm People of neither Property or significance among us."[28]

Galloway's name headed the Committee on Observation chosen by the "few warm People" to carry out the recommendations of the Continental Congress. There were twenty-eight others, their names significant if their property was not: names that were Irish, German, English, French, Scottish. They were men whom Galloway could have influenced and led; they had shown their respect for him by placing him at the head of the committee. But, from his point of view, they

[28] Galloway to Verplanck, dated at "Trevor" [sic], Jan. 14, 1774 [1775]; *Penn. Mag. Hist. and Biog.*, XXI. 478.

were not only insignificant and propertyless: they were dangerous to government, inimical to the interests of a ruling, propertied class, and very probably meant to set themselves up as a petty tyranny of the uninformed and the licentious. Galloway believed firmly, though his metaphors were confused, "that we are on the brink of a Precipice 'big with the fate of America.' "[29] His answer to this fateful issue, though, was not to seek a solution within the extra-legal framework set up by his neighbors, guiding and influencing them by his superior talents.

One seeks in vain through the somewhat solemn proceedings of the Bucks County Committee of Safety for evidences of the tyranny of the people that Galloway so much feared. Here, in embryo, perhaps no worse and no better in Bucks County than elsewhere, was one of the genuine creative acts of the Revolution, the impressive spectacle of a free people groping cautiously but determinedly for the forms of government that would enable them to defend their rights as freemen. It was "with the greatest Decency and Harmony" that the Bucks County Committee of Safety first met on July 9, 1774, to consider what should be done by "Americans . . . subjected to the universal controul of a Legislature in which they are not represented." Perhaps Galloway had participated in that meeting. Certainly the resolutions there adopted were in accord with his views and almost in his words:

Resolved, That the inhabitants of this Country have the same opinion of the dangerous tendency of the Claims of the British Parliament to make laws, binding on the inhabitants of these Colonies in all Cases whatsoever, without their consent, as other of our fellow American subjects have. . . . That it is the duty of every American, when oppressed by measures either of Ministry, Parliament, or any other Power, to use every lawful endeavour to obtain relief, and to form and promote a Plan of Union between the parent country and colonies in which the claim of the parent country may be ascertained and the Liberties of the Colonies

[29] *Ibid.,* XXI. 484.

defined and secured, and no Cause of Contention in future may arise to disturb that Harmony so necessary for the interest and happiness of both. . . .[30]

In November the Committee approved the actions of the Continental Congress, but in January declined—as Galloway had predicted—to participate in the Provincial Congress called by the Philadelphia Committee, since they could not "conceive from any information we had had, the necessity of such Provincial Convention or that any good effects can be produced thereby towards carrying into execution the Association so clearly pointed out to us by the Continental Congress." Not until after Lexington and Concord did the committee conclude that, "notwithstanding the disapprobation we have hitherto shown to the prosecution of any violent measures of opposition," attempts were being made to carry "the oppressive Acts of Parliament into execution by military force" and therefore the people should form themselves into militia companies so as to be "capable of affording their Country that aid which its particular necessitys may at any time require."

Even so, these defensive measures were conducted with order and a rather scrupulous regard for democratic procedures. Money was collected for the inhabitants of Boston on a voluntary basis, properly transmitted to John or Samuel Adams, and carefully accounted for by signed vouchers. Doubtless there were instances of mob pressure; certainly there were the familiar compulsions of family or group opinion. But if out-of-doors sanctions were used, the degree of violence or petty tyranny exercised by the Committee is perhaps best gauged by official actions of the committee in dealing with those who were disaffected to their country's cause. Various inhabitants were represented to the Committee as having "uttered expressions derogatory to the Continental Congress and inimicable to the Liberties of America."[31] Some

[30] *Ibid.*, XV. 258*ff*.
[31] The first was on July 21, 1775; *ibid.*, XV. 263.

of these inhabitants were brought before the committee; most of them made retractions; some promised to support the efforts to redress American grievances so long as those efforts were consistent with their religious scruples. One Thomas Smith had declared

That the Measures of Congress had already enslaved America and done more damage than all the Acts of Parliament ever intended to lay upon us, that the whole was nothing but a scheme of a parcel of hot-headed Presbyterians and that he believed the Devil was at the bottom of the whole; that the taking up Arms was the most scandalous thing a man could be guilty of, and more heinous than an hundred of the grossest offences against the moral law, &c. &c. &c.[32]

Proceeding on "incontestable evidence" that Smith had made these remarks, the committee imposed the most severe penalty among all its acts down to the summer of 1776: "That . . . the said Thomas Smith be considered as an Enemy to the Rights of British America, and that all persons break off every kind of dealing with him until he shall make proper satisfaction to this Committee for his misconduct." Less than three weeks later Smith expressed "remorse and penitence" and promised to support "every measure prosecuted for the redress of American Grievances so far as is consistent with the religious principles of the society to which I belong." This promise of qualified support the Committee accepted as a sufficient satisfaction. The clerk of the committee had sent the facts of the Smith case to the press, but when he appeared penitent, their publication was postponed. As this was the worst offense and the worst penalty, so others were beneath the notice of the Committee: once with an obvious sense of its own dignity, the Committee resolved that "the offence as well as the offender are too insignificant to deserve any further notice of this Committee." At the end of a year's service the Committee, "being of opinion a new choice ought to be annually made," called for a new election,

[32] *Ibid.*, XV. 266.

with the result that only seven out of the original twenty-nine members of the committee were returned to serve for the year 1776. Several members who had been elected in 1774 had declined to serve; others had served but "from Scruples of Conscience made application to be discharged." The Committee's only answer to this was to "request all those who do not propose attending for the future to advertise their respective townships with their determination, at the same time appointing some convenient time and place for the inhabitants to meet, and choose other suitable persons in their room. . . ." Such were the official acts of the men who, with those who were taking similar steps throughout the British colonies in America, held the answers to the questions raised by the momentous months from 1774 to 1776.

Had a Washington, a Jefferson, a Lee, or an Adams lived at Trevose in those fateful months, the weight of his influence probably would have been brought to bear upon his neighbors. In the winter of 1774-75 the balance of the scales was not yet tipped toward independence. The issue was still a political issue; the lines were drawn between political factions, not between belligerents—Thomas Smith was an enemy, not of America, but of "the Rights of *British* America." But, fearing that the actions of the Congress and of the Committees of Safety would lead to excesses, to leveling ideas, to the disturbance of law and order, Galloway withdrew from active participation in the councils of his neighbors. On his return from New York in December, fortified in his convictions by association with the conservatives of New York, he decided to speak plainly. "When I went to the Assembly," he wrote Verplanck,

and found they had approved of the measures of the Congress so fully, and had appointed me one of the Delegates at the next, I very explicitly told them, that I entirely disapproved of them. I did so in Congress and continued yet of the same opinion and that I might not appear to undertake the Execution of measures which my judgment and conscience disapproved of I could not serve them as a Delegate in the ensuing Congress.[33]

Closing the door even more firmly, Galloway began in December or January to prepare a pamphlet arraigning the measures of the first Congress. "When I began it, I was in a low state of Health, and by the Time I had finished it," he told Verplanck,

so much unwell with a fever and colic, as to be altogether unable to correct or copy my first thoughts. This induced me at Times, to think of delaying the Publication, But the necessity that called for it, and a Belief that it will be of use, has induced me to run the risk of critical censures for the Public Good, being confident that the Principles and Doctrines are sound and irrefragable.[34]

Fever and colic, exacerbating an already embittered mind, may have had a greater effect on Galloway's future and on the distant fate of his irrefragable doctrines than he suspected.

The *Candid Examination of the Mutual Claims of Great Britain* was published by James Rivington in February 1775. Professing the desire to avoid alike the advocacy of the American position which deduced rights from the law of nature or made distinctions between internal and external taxes—"Distinctions which never existed, but in the wild imagination of the authors of them"—and the advocacy of Parliamentary supremacy which contended for the right "to exercise absolute power over the lives, liberties, and properties, of three millions of British subjects," Galloway sought the answers where he considered none had looked before: in "the fundamental laws of the British constitution, where only *the rights of that authority*, and *the privileges of the subject*, are defined and ascertained." This was a laudable purpose: but Galloway's first paragraph nullified any chance of conciliatory effect on the minds of his countrymen. He saw America

governed by the barbarian rule of frantic folly, and lawless ambi-

[33]*Ibid.*, XXI. 477-78.

[45]

tion . . . freedom of speech suppressed, the liberty and secrecy of the press destroyed, the voice of truth silenced; a lawless power established throughout the Colonies, forming laws for the government of their conduct, depriving men of their natural rights, and inflicting penalties more severe than death itself, upon a disobedience to their edicts . . . the Colonies, needlessly . . . pushing on with precipitation and madness, in the high-road of sedition and rebellion. . . .

After this, Galloway's intention to review "the most important controversy that ever was agitated between a State and its Members" in the hope that his countrymen, "too long seduced from their true interest, by false, though specious arguments, will, at length, listen to reason and truth," was worse than wasted time. It served no purpose, beyond that of inflaming the "lawless power," to review his efforts in Congress to promote a conciliatory Plan of Union, and to publish that plan, while impugning the motives of the members of Congress. If frantic folly was abroad in the land, Galloway won no converts by describing it as such.

Nor was his simplification of the issue convincing to those Americans who, erroneously or not, based their cause on the natural rights of man: in all governments one all-pervading, universal principle was found to operate—Locke's "first fundamental positive law of all commonwealth's," the supremacy of the legislative power which was to be "sacred and unalterable in the hands where the community have placed it." No one could deny that such a power had been established in "the British Society," lodged in the King, Lords, and Commons. To those who claimed an equality of legislative status in the American colonies and who protested, as Wilson did, that they were joined in the empire only by allegiance to the Crown, Galloway replied: if this was allegiance to the King of England, it involved an allegiance also to the laws created by the legislative authority of which the King was a part; if it was allegiance to the King in America, "when did he assume that title and by whom was it conferred?" Thus, it followed, the supreme legislative authority must extend to all members of the government, or else those members were "so many independent communities, in a state of nature, with respect to it." Parliament, Galloway continued, had exercised its supremacy over the colonies since their first settlement, and the colonies had yielded proper obedience to that supreme authority. But in their late declaration of rights in Congress, their denial of Parliamentary authority was grounded on the "immutable laws of nature."

But John Locke was an abundant arsenal furnishing ammunition to both sides in this momentous battle in the realm of government. If he argued for a supreme legislative authority controlling all members of the State, so did he believe that this authority itself was bound by the higher law of nature not to infringe rights of life, liberty, property, and equality. If such rights were infringed by the supreme legislative authority, then its positive laws were tyranny and usurpation. When this happened, the people could then exercise their right, guaranteed by the law of God and nature, of revolution.[35] But this was the sort of logic that was more useful to John Adams than to Joseph Galloway, and while the latter appealed to Locke in arguing for supremacy of Parliament, he parted company with him when he revered natural law. Preferring Mansfield, Camden, and Blackstone, Galloway argued that natural law was founded upon the principles of "reason and immutable justice, which require a rigid performance of every lawful contract."[36] To suppose, therefore, "that a right can thence be derived, to violate the most solemn and sacred of all covenants [the establishment of the supreme legislative authority]; those upon which the welfare of millions depends; is, in the highest degree, absurd." What was worse, a denial of that supremacy by subjects caused them to forfeit "not only their right to the

[34] Feb. 14, 1775; *ibid.*, XXI. 480.
[35] *Of Civil Government*, Bk. ii, chs. iv, v, ix, xi, xix.
[36] *Candid Examination* (London, 1780), 29.

[47]

protection of the State, but every other right or claim under it." Congress, therefore, besides being an irregular and illegal body, had forfeited American rights. Fully unmasked, therefore, the aim of "the delegates of North America . . . appears to be that of absolute independency on the Mother State." To be sure, America had rights which it was to the interest of the parent state to respect. These rights, however, could be protected only by some plan of constitutional union such as the one Galloway had proposed and the Congress had disregarded.

The *Candid Examination* met with the approval of Samuel Verplanck and Galloway's other friends in New York. Others in Pennsylvania welcomed it, and the author found it "decried by none but Independents, or such as are determined to bring about a total separation of the two countries at all events, and they are, you may be assured, but one fourth Part of our People."[37] Among the latter was John Dickinson, who promptly published *An Address to the Author of the Pamphlet*, asserting the doctrine—later to become imbedded in the structure of the American government—that in their spheres of jurisdiction the local legislatures were as supreme as was Parliament within its sphere. This Galloway repudiated in his *Reply to an Address* as impossible and utterly discordant with the universal principle in government of a supreme legislature. Dickinson's pamphlet, Galloway affirmed in a letter to Verplanck, was

the Production of a fortnight Labour of the Pennsylvania Farmer and his old Assistant Charles Thompson. From the little approbation it met with here, I should not have thought it worthy a Reply, But it gave me an opportunity of explaining some Principles of the Pamphlet [*Candid Examination*] more fully—And besides I thought that the vanity and Ignorance of the Author ought to be exposed.

If the *Candid Examination* was intemperate, the *Reply to*

[37] *Penn. Mag. of Hist. and Biog.*, XXI. 481-82.

an Address permanently eliminated the author as a conciliatory influence in America. "Perhaps there is in it too much
acrimony," Galloway admitted, "and yet I think they deserve it."[38]

The *Candid Examination*, he declared later, "was circulated throughout America, and had a considerable degree of
influence on the minds of the people in general; but it was
for that reason destroyed by the Independent party, whenever they could find it, and in several provinces it was burnt
by the common executioner." And when the reply to Dickinson's pamphlet was advertised, "a party of the Independents
from Connecticut came down on the day of its publication,
destroyed and carried off his printing materials, drove him
into exile, and finally suppressed the liberty of the press
throughout America."[39] This, at least, was Galloway's recollection in 1780; but the Sons of Liberty of Connecticut must
have been slow to anger—for the *Reply to An Address* was
sent to Rivington in March, probably published in April,
and the destructive raid on his plant came on November 27.[40]

But long before that date Galloway had made himself rep-
rehensible to those whom he called Independents. "On Thurs-
day & Friday last," as he wrote to William Franklin on February 28, 1775,

determined to abide the Consequences what ever they might be
either in respect to my Person or Estate, I spoke my Sentiments in
Assembly without the least reserve. I censured & condemned the
Measures of the Congress in every Thing—aver'd that they all
tended to incite America to sedition & terminated in Independence—contended for & proved the Necessity of Parliamentary
Jurisdiction over the Colonies in all Cases whatsoever—exposed
the Folly of those who hoped, that the British State would suffer
its Authority to be in the least impaired, much less totally given

[38] *Ibid.*, XXI. 482.
[39] London edition, 1780, vi.
[40] I am indebted to Dr. Victor H. Paltsits for calling my attention to the
statement in Rivington's *New York Gazetteer* of April 6, 1775, that the *Reply
to an Address* was "In the Press, and speedily will be published."

up—explained the rights of America; & pointed out the Necessity of our taking different Measures from those already taken for a recovery of them. I stood single & unsupported, among a Set of Men every one of whom had approved of the Measures I was censuring. . . .[41]

William Allen, John Dickinson, Charles Thomson, Thomas Mifflin, and George Ross battered the abandoned leader of the Assembly in what he thought was a "violent & indecent" attack. By autumn his defection had spread abroad, and on October 1 Ezra Stiles of Yale recorded in his diary: "Mr. Galloway has . . . fallen from a great height into contempt and infamy; but he never was entirely confided in as a thorough son of liberty." Within another year he had put himself under the protection of the British army. Having alienated the confidence of his countrymen in America, he thenceforth addressed his thoughts on imperial reorganization to British ears.

[41] *N. J. Arch.*, X. 573-74.

CHAPTER IV

PRELUDE TO A SYSTEM OF POLICY

MANY YEARS LATER Galloway wrote that the Plan of Union he had presented to the Continental Congress of 1774 was "founded in the liberty and safety of both" England and America.

Its great principle was, that no law should bind America without her consent. I wished it might be made the basis of negotiation and peace, and declared, as many must recollect, that if the principle should not be granted by the British State, I would embark my life and fortune to obtain it. It was thought so reasonable and supported by so many Gentlemen of abilities that it was referred by Congress for further consideration. It was, however, never considered—military measures were immediately after adopted, and soon after independence declared. I had repeatedly taken the Qualification of allegiance to the King of Great Britain, and I could not prevail on myself to act contrary to them until the measure I then believed would be productive of peace had been assayed [*sic*] and rejected. Besides the dreadful consequences and uncertain events of a war I concluded would ultimately prove the ruin of America. Nor was I singular in that opinion. Under these impressions I retired to the country resolved neither to influence the opinion of others; nor to give the least opposition myself to the measures adopted. This determination I religiously observed. But, altho' at this time I had given no just offence to any, what was my situation? It cannot be forgotten by many in Philadelphia. My life, during several months, was in perpetual jeopardy. Every night I expected would be my last. Men were excited by some persons from the northward, by falsehoods fabricated for the purpose, to put me to death. Several attempts were made, but providentially prevented before the execution. I declared my innocence in the public papers in vain. There was nothing during that time to impede my joining the British forces. But, altho' the preservation of life dictated the Measure, I would not, preferring danger to safety on those terms. At length an order was made by the Executive Council to arrest me for high treason. Desponding now of any possible safety, I fled to New-Jersey where I remained some time hesitating to join the British, and unwilling to act against America. But finding there was no other asylum I was by unavoidable necessity driven into the measure. From this time on, and not before, I took a decided part.[1]

This, at least, was Galloway's recollection in 1793 when he was making his last futile attempt to return to America. Under such circumstances, strict accuracy is not to be expected. Had he not been so prominent in provincial politics, had he not made so many enemies by his fights with the Proprietors and with Dickinson, it is possible that, like William Samuel Johnson in Connecticut or Joseph Wanton in Rhode Island or Daniel Dulany in Maryland or some of the Allens in Pennsylvania, he would have been permitted to live a quietly neutral existence during the turmoil of war. Some neutrals, and among them some very able men, were so treated. But Galloway was scarcely neutral in the months following the meeting of the Continental Congress. Many of those in Philadelphia in 1793 no doubt did recollect Galloway's Plan of Union of 1774, but more of them remembered the violence of his *Candid Examination*. It was doubtless remembered also that, while he had signed the non-importation agreement as a member of Congress, he had impeded its execution as an individual, justifying the inconsistency by saying that he had signed it only in his official capacity as a representative. Others may have remembered that early in 1775 he had publicly accused a committee of the Assembly, including Dickinson and Charles Thomson, of acting "a dishonorable, disingenuous dirty and fraudulent part, one unbecoming men in public character."[2] They remembered also the box that had been sent to Galloway with

[1] To Thomas McKean, March 7, 1793; McKean Papers, Hist. Soc. of Pa., II. 108.
[2] *N. J. Arch.*, 1st. ser., X. 579*ff*.

[52]

a halter in it, together with an insurance policy that he would not be alive in six days, and a note reading: "Hang yourself or we shall do it for you."[3] Perhaps they remembered the lines in Trumbull's *M'Fingal* about Galloway:

> What ropes and halters did you send
> Terrific emblems of his end,
> Till, least he'd hang in more than effigy
> Fled in a fog the trembling refugee?

They remembered, no doubt, the charges that Galloway had sent information to the British ministry, and remembered— or disbelieved—Galloway's firm denial in the *Pennsylvania Gazette* that he "directly or indirectly . . . ever wrote a sentiment to any man in Great Britain injurious to the rights and freedom of America, nor ever recommended any measure whatever to be persued in respect to the present dispute between the two countries."[4] This was published six months after he had sent the Plan of Union to William Franklin and exactly two months after he had sent his last letter to Franklin, which Franklin forwarded to Dartmouth with the statement that his informant "will, most probably, be entirely ignorant of my Intentions of communicating it to His Majesty or his Ministers."

Nor was it the attainder of treason (which did not come until 1778) that precipitated Galloway's flight, but probably the arrival of the British in New York and General Howe's proclamation of amnesty on November 30, 1776. A Philadelphia versifier, who may have been Francis Hopkinson, announced Galloway's defection:[5]

> Galloway has fled and joined the venal Howe
> To prove his baseness, see him cringe and bow.
> A traitor to his country and its laws
> A friend to tyrants and their cursed cause

. . . .

[3] *Penn. Mag. of Hist. and Biog.*, XXVI. 430.

[4] *Ibid.*, XXVI. 431; *Pa. Gazette*, May 12, 1775.

[5] Baldwin, *op. cit.*, XXVI. 433, citing Moore's *Diary of the Revolution*, I. 369.

There herd with Bute, Mansfield, and his brother,
Bite, twist, sting, and poison one another.

It was not with Bute or Mansfield that Galloway herded, but with a young Englishman, Ambrose Serle, former secretary to the Earl of Dartmouth and now secretary to Admiral Howe. Serle, even though his principal interest later in life was Calvinist theology, immediately gained the respect of Galloway, who was ten years his senior. Serle, as secretary to the Earl of Dartmouth, already knew about Galloway because of the secret letters that the latter had sent through William Franklin to the secretary of state. They met in New York on December 31, 1776, and Serle recorded his opinion of the Pennsylvania Loyalist in his diary: "He fully answers the Idea of good Sense and Integrity I had entertained of him from his confidential Correspondence in England." Like William Allen, who had been with Serle the evening before, Galloway thought "the Power of the Rebellion is pretty well broken."[6] During the succeeding months the young Englishman and the Pennsylvania Loyalist spent many evenings together, sometimes with other Loyalists from New York, New Jersey, and Pennsylvania, and they found that their views respecting Plans of Union for the future government of the colonies were remarkably similar. The more they agreed, the more highly they esteemed one another. "I saw Mr. Galloway this Morning," wrote Serle a week after their first meeting, "& am much pleased with his solid Sense & thorough Knowledge of American Politics." The next day they compared their "Plans of accomodation, and agreed entirely in Sentiment; This wd have been the Case with a few honest men treating on both Sides."[7]

What Serle meant by "honest men," of course, was men who agreed as thoroughly as he and Galloway agreed. Noth-

[6] Edward H. Tatum, Jr., ed., *The American Journal of Ambrose Serle, Secretary to Lord Howe, 1776-1778* (San Marino, 1940), 165.
[7] *Ibid.*, 171.

ing, as Serle, Galloway, Inglis, Allen and others of like sentiment amply demonstrated, could be quite so complete as the
agreement of partisans defending the established order
against subversive forces. Protected by the weight of tradi-
tion, bound together by a common respect for established
authority, united in regard for what, with all its faults,
seemed an excellent social order in its gentility, its wealth,
and its culture, and insulated against ideas and men who
threatened that order, the Loyalists who thronged New York
in the winter of 1776 incubated ideas of a remarkable
sameness.

The pattern of their thought was a well-worn groove.
Serle himself, in 1775, had published a pamphlet which
might have been written by Galloway: *Americans against
Liberty; or, an Essay on the Nature and Principles of True
Freedom, Shewing that the Designs and Conduct of the
Americans Tend only to Tyranny and Slavery.*[8] The Kings,
Lords, and Commons were the supreme authority under the
British constitution. This being so, there could not be, in
theory or in fact, two or more legislative authorities of equal
rank. If it were asserted, the constitution, "so long the admiration of the world," would fall into ruin. Every member
of the empire was born under this supreme authority, was
subject to it and received protection from it. Thus disposed of
by constitutional dialectic, the "rebel Americans, in the wild-
est delusion and by the worst means, are avowing themselves
the open enemies to the public and general liberty of the
British Empire." Independence, plainly, had been their object from the beginning. And why were they so lacking in
gratitude for the blessings of such a constitution, for the
country whose navy had made them powerful and had protected them against the common enemy? "Debts to English
merchants, smuggling, and the total relaxation of government
have laid the foundation of all the present rebellion." The
parent state, giving its protection, had been drained of men

[8] London, 1775.

and wealth in the settlement of the colonies, and in return it had received only competition in industry and trade, debts that were seldom paid, and outright disloyalty. Philadelphia, Boston, and New York were thriving examples of the energy that had been drawn from the mother country. Nevertheless, though the colonies had become too strong commercially for the good of the empire, too independent in religion, and far too democratic in politics, some system could and should be adopted to "bring them and keep them from abroad into a closed union and dependence with the parent state." This would have to be preceded by force, for a mutual agreement would not serve: the professions of attachment of the Americans could not be depended upon "farther than we have the power to command it," and such a settlement would only postpone the day of reckoning until the time when the colonies would become too powerful. The rebellion must, therefore, be crushed, and then a constitution could be "conferred with grace and with dignity, as from the supreme power of the state." Under such a constitution, the colonial legislatures could not be permitted to decide questions which might "affect the very being of the empire without in effect raising several paltry independent states from the ruins of one great political and commercial body." Such a reorganization of the empire should include an established church in order to counteract the leveling tendencies of Presbyterian republicans, limitations on immigration should be established, and naturalization of aliens in the colonies should be abolished.

The character and motives of American leaders constituted another bond of agreement between Serle and Galloway and other conservatives.[9] Those leaders, they were convinced, were a small band of self-seeking men who had imposed their wills on the people for well-concealed ends. Their rise to leadership, unaccompanied by the usual marks of gentility or evidences of a governing class, could be ex-

[9] Tatum, *op. cit.*, 25, 31, 46-47, 121-22, 149.

plained in no other way, for British officialdom and British-American conservatives recognized no other system of leadership. General Sullivan had begun his career as a menial servant. Roger Sherman had been a cobbler. General Putnam was scarcely literate. Benjamin Franklin had been a printer. General Heath was a butcher. Governor Trumbull waited his turn in the village barber shop like a common subject, not as if he were the head of a government. Could such men govern from any other motives than self-interest, or could the people respect such leaders except they were deceived? That sort of leadership had unbridled the dangerous democratic spirit, and government therefore "must acquire a new Energy in this Country, and the democratic Principle be more controuled." Nothing was plainer to the conservatives than that "Mobs, or rather two or three worthless Fellows at the Head of the Mobs, have ruled every thing in this Country of late Years, in Defiance of all Law, Order, and Humanity." "In the new Constitution of Things," consequently, Britain would have to set up in the colonies some provision for hereditary honors.

By the middle of January 1777, Galloway and Serle got down seriously to the business of which they never tired, a new constitution for the empire. "We perfectly agreed in opinion," wrote Serle on the twenty-ninth, "that nothing but a new Constitution, analogous to & co-ordinate with the Constitution of Britain, will settle & secure the Colonies." They also agreed perfectly that, unless this were done, Great Britain would in a short while be stripped of her colonies, and America, unsettled and disputing within itself, would become "first a Field of Blood, and then the Domain of some arbitrary Despot at the Head of an Army." On such matters, Serle concluded, "I never met a man, with whom I could more perfectly agree in Politics than Mr. G[alloway]. nor one, who more coolly investigates the Causes and Order of public Affairs." But how was this new constitution to be arrived at, "by Colonies *singulatim*, or with the Continent as a

[57]

whole . . . by a Constitution formed upon Treaty here with Delegates from the Assemblies, &c. or by one conceded by G. Britain & framed with the advice of some intelligent People of this Country, sent home for that Purpose, by the King in Parliament"? Obviously not by treaty, for the word of Americans would be binding only so long as their interests or their fears dictated. America must first be brought into a state of submission, and, while the army remained in the colonies to keep order, "a Constitution free and just in itself, analogous to & co-ordinate with that of Britain, should be generously granted to this Country, and accordingly be previously prepared for it, with the advice of some intelligent Americans, upon its several Parts." The colonial assemblies might "propose any Amendment of Defects, Alterations, or Additions, which if concurred in by the British Legislature shall become Part of the Constitution: That this Constitution, finally recognized by Deputies from the Respective Assemblies, shall be the Constitution and *Magna Charta* of the Colonies, unalterable but by the joint Consent & mutual agreement of them & their Mother-Country." Such was the proposal that came out of a conversation between Charles Inglis, Joseph Galloway, and Ambrose Serle on March 10, 1777, a conversation, Serle thought, which resulted in their feeling "extremely satisfied with each other."[10] Implicit in all their complacent discussion was the unspoken assumption that the Old Empire was a good and worthy institution, that an empire bound together by the ledgers and journals of traders and by the British navy could be continued only if the supreme power of Parliament were recognized throughout its extent, and that force, if need be, was the ultimate sanction of such a supremacy. That assumption Serle and Galloway did not think of questioning.

But Serle and Galloway, continuing with unflagging enthusiasm their wearisome repetition of the old theme while Washington avoided coming to grips with Howe, were not

[10] *Ibid.*, 181, 194, 198-99.

content with their parlor theorizing. With the spring of 1777 they decided to lay their ideas before high officials of the home government, and in March Galloway began work on a draft of what he regarded as "a Necessary Prelude to a System of Policy." This he decided to cast in the form of a letter to Richard Jackson, Solicitor to the Board of Trade, King's Counsel, and wise ally of Franklin and Galloway in the days when they were attacking the Proprietary government of Pennsylvania. Serle wrote in his journal on March 21, 1777, that he

Had some very Confidential Conversation with Mr. G[alloway]. on the Subject of public affairs. He shewed, & promised me the Copy of, a Lr. written by him to Mr. Jackson, wch contains his Sentiments & my own on the *manner* of the Settlemt. The *Time* we also discussed, and agreed, that when the Colonies were brought to Submission, instead of declaring them at Peace *immediately*, let the *new* Constitution be promulged, and every thing be settled *at once*, by *Parliament*. Our Sentiments perfectly coincided upon this most important matter, wch, I believe, we both of us have closely at Heart for the Honor Happiness & Welfare of the whole Empire. *Nunc redime tempus, post est occasio calva.*[11]

Two days later Serle noted that he had received "a very important and sensible [letter] . . . to a Gentleman in London."[12] Galloway had never met Jackson, but in his letter of March 20 he wrote as to an old friend and correspondent:

I am yet at New York endeavouring to be of Service to those entrusted with the great Work of reclaiming my Countrymen from their Delusion, and restoring them to the Peace of their Sovereign and Bosom of their Mother Country; and I have reason to believe my Information has not been entirely useless or inacceptable. [Galloway had submitted to Lord Howe a plan for securing forage and had told Serle that it was approved.] The Winter has been spent in Skirmishes between . . . the British foraging Parties and detached corps of the Rebels. The former

[11] *Ibid.*, 201.
[12] *Ibid.*, 202.

have always had the Advantage, never failing to push and rout the latter. [But now the spring campaign was about to open, and he hoped that the reduction of America would soon be effected.] For, what with the continued Tyranny of the Congress, Committees and the new Independent States—The Pillage, Robberies and Inhumanity of the Rebel Army—the vigorous Operations of the Fleet under Lord Howe, in cutting off the military supplies, the conveniences and necessaries of Life, and added to the Successes of the Army under Sir William Howe, such a rapid Change in the Opinions and Dispositions of the Americans has taken Place, that another Campaign will, in all Probability, put an End to the Rebellion.[13]

When this imminent event took place, what would be done next? As a friend to both countries, as one who wished to conclude his days in America and to leave his country and posterity happy after him, Galloway was anxiously concerned that something should be done as soon as possible to bind both countries together "in Bonds of the most permanent Policy." There had been a time, Galloway argued, when such a plan of accommodation was impossible, and he clearly had in mind his own Plan of 1774:

A violent Opposition to Government at Home—the Nation divided in Opinion on the Subject—the Views of America *concealed* in false Pretences and unknown—Her Pride unbounded—An Opinion of her Wealth and Resources extravagant—and her Ambition to be independent utterly incontroulable by Reason and Argument: All these were so many insuperable Obstacles to any reasonable Plan of Accomodation between the two Countries.

But now all was reversed, or so it seemed to the Loyalists who crowded each other's dinner tables in New York City and outdid themselves to show their unanimity of opinion: Great Britain was at peace with all the world, her Opposition party was non-existent, America had shown her hand openly, and had exposed her cherished design of independence.

[13] *B. F. Stevens's Facsimiles of Manuscripts in European Archives Relating to America.* Nos. 2051 and 2055; Hist. MSS Com., *Fourteenth Report,* Appendix, Part X, 435, 436-37.

The Pride and Ambition of the Colonies humbled by . . . [England's] Power—Their republican Demagogues dispersed and lost to all influence—their People, reclaimed and enlightened by the never failing Arguments of severe Distress, brought on them by the Tyranny of their Leaders and their own Folly—and made sensible of their former Liberty and Happiness, and their present Slavery and Misery—and of the lenity of that Government against which they have rebel'd and of the Necessity of Order and Subordination—Under these Circumstances America will be ready to submit, with Chearfulness, without Opposition or Murmur, to any just and reasonable Constitution that shall be offer'd.

Had not the time arrived, then, or must it not soon arrive, "for establishing that System of Policy which shall restore the disjointed Members of the Empire and bring them within that Circle of Power and Influence, that can alone attach and cement them to the Principal State and secure their Obedience for Ages to come?"

Galloway, full of optimistic hope engendered by constant association with Loyalists as embittered, as disillusioned, and as insulated against realities as he was, saw the issue in terms of simple logic. His assumption granted, the solution lay clearly marked out. He was glad now that the Plan of Union of 1774 had been rejected.

The Several Attempts & Propositions . . . [such as that Plan, were] so inadequate to a perfect and lasting Incorporation, that I have often thought it fortunate they were not adopted. They were only Plaisters which might have suddenly skin'd over the Wound, but woud certainly have left it corroding and mortifying within, to break out at a future Period, and not a very distant one, with redoubled, and perhaps incurable Violence. They were formed on a Sudden, and without Information or due Deliberation. The Disaster was not traced to its original Sources, nor its Causes unfolded. No wonder then that the Remedies prescribed were improper, and that the Cure would not have been radical.

Changing his metaphor, Galloway thought that the seeds of rebellion were of many kinds and had been planted in different soils, but they all would have eventually flowered into the dangerous maturity of rebellion. They were concealed in religious principles, in the variety of forms of the colonial governments, in the independence of the officers of the Crown and their reliance on popular favor, in the want of civil discipline, in an almost totally lax administration of the laws, in want of respect for the supreme authority of the state, and in a too great inattention in government to the colonies since their foundation. Changing his metaphor once more, Galloway suggested to Jackson that if these causes of rebellion were duly considered, there could be no doubt that "the Diamond might be found in this Heap of Rubbish, upon which a Constitution might be reard, that shall bind the Colonies to the Mother State and Secure their Dependence in future Ages."

If done at all, this must be done by Parliament, and Parliament alone. There were precedents to justify it, and the method would be legal and constitutional. If Great Britain decided, on the other hand, to await proposals for an imperial constitution from America, there would be a disastrous delay. How would they be obtained, and would they come from the several distinct colonies? If so, there would be such a variety of perplexing plans, so dissimilar and so conflicting, that there would not only be delay, but it would be "impossible ever to arrange them into any just and permanent system." Every colony would be prejudiced in favor of its own plan, and if it should be rejected and another chosen, "Disgust perhaps will take Place and a Foundation be laid for Future Discord." If, on the other hand, the proposed constitution was to come from a general American congress, "a commission must be issued to render their meeting legal." Even so, "after they have deliberated on the Subject, American Ideas of Liberty and Policy which have been very bady digested, as late Experience has shown, will prevail. Should they be improper and inadmissible, many Difficulties will arise, and how are they to be settled (if ever settled at all) in any reasonable time between Persons at three thousand miles Distance from each other, and only convened once in a Year?" Nothing seemed more clearly demonstrable to Galloway than that American ideas of liberty would come out of an American congress, or that they would be inadmissible in any "plan of accommodation." Accommodation, to the suffering Loyalist, really meant not the adjustment of ideas and the composing of differences, but the imposition of "that Circle of Power and Influence" of which Galloway had written.

Moreover, Galloway added, to permit America to initiate the proposal for a new constitution for the empire, would "give Life to that Ambition which now lies buried in the Ashes of her Reduction." To permit her the right of negotiating by treaty would be placing inferior members of the state on a par with the supreme power, "whereas by the Constitution already settled they can have a Right only to Petition or remonstrate and not to treat." Parliament, therefore, should initiate the matter, acquire information, investigate the causes of the revolt, and "establish *by its own Authority* such a System as shall give the same Constitution, Laws, Manners & Freedom, *or as nearly the same as may be,* to the People in America as are possessed and enjoyed by their Brethren in Britain." When this was done, let it be given to America for her government and executed immediately. It would be submitted to without opposition or murmur by the colonies, "when the Spirit of this Ambition is effectually subdued, and their Reason awakened by their Distress."

If, however, this method should develop inconveniences or errors in operation, then the colonies "will Petition for Amendment and Parliament will Amend. Thus this great work will be accomplished in a regular and Constitutional Mode. And it will be done in the most *expeditious, easiest, safest,* and *best* manner. Every other Mode seems 'puzzled with mazes & perplexed Errors,' which lead to Difficulties not

[63]

to be surmounted." But whatever the mode, a perfect incorporation with the British government was essential. It was the want of such a principle that had nearly destroyed the Roman empire, and it was, Galloway thought, the adoption of this principle by which "all the wide extended Parts of that Empire were reconciled and restored to Peace—and its Colonies ever after steady in their Obedience, lived and expired with the Empire itself."

Though Galloway said later that this letter to Richard Jackson was thrown together in haste, it was nevertheless the product of over two months' thought and conversation with Serle and others, and it showed some deliberation by the preparation of a preliminary draft. By the same packet that carried it to Jackson, Ambrose Serle enclosed a copy of it in a letter to Lord Dartmouth, dated March 25, 1777.

I thought, [he wrote] the Sentiments of this sensible Man, who has perhaps the largest Influence, if not Fortune, of any one Person in these Colonies, might be at least a Matter of Curiosity to Your Lordship. He talks of visiting England, for the first Time, after the next campaign. Nobody perhaps could be consulted with, to more Advantage to the Public; and nobody with less View to his own, separate from the Public. I am happy in his acquaintance; which is a Truth I can say of but few Americans.

The substance of the letter was put by Serle in the form of a postscript:

Mr. Galloway, who has a very high Respect for Your Lordship, has particularly intimated to me his Wish, that his Thoughts upon this momentous Crisis might be communicated to Your Lordship and to Lord North, if You approve them. His Heart seems much engaged in the *permanent* Settlement of these Affairs, on the Success of which his large Property is entirely staked. I need not add to Your Lordship, that his Abilities and Character are of the very first Rate in this Country; nor need I say, with how much good Policy and Effect they may be used upon a proper Occasion.[14]

---

[14] *Stevens's Facsimiles*, No. 2053.

On March 28, 1777, since the packet carrying Galloway's letter of March 20 had not sailed, Galloway added another to Richard Jackson. He had heard of the appointment of a Commission by the North ministry to entertain proposals for conciliation, and he felt that, in a dispute respecting the powers of Parliament, it would be prejudicial to do anything more than to offer and receive proposals. And at any rate, he felt that the objects which gave rise to the commission were now entirely lost. The colonies had denied "all the Rights of Parliament and of the Crown," had declared themselves independent, civil war had taken place, and had resulted in the reduction of America. "By this reduction America has forfeited all her Rights, and now remains a Chart Blanche upon which the Parliament may write and establish such a Plan of lasting Policy as shall give Freedom to the Colonists and secure their Obedience in Time to come." Every colonial government was now dissolved—"dissolved by the Americans themselves, and not only dissolved but upon every Principle of Law forfeited, and the Charter Governments not only by the People living under them, but by the Grantees and Proprietors themselves. No legislatures and no Representatives of the People are in being." The people of America could not, therefore, entertain legal proposals or make agreements binding upon themselves without restoring every colony to its former plan of government. And this, Galloway contended, would merely reëstablish many of the causes of rebellion and prevent the alterations in colonial governments that were so much needed. But government, he was satisfied, would see the need for reducing all of the colonies to a similar plan of government, for such a favorable opportunity for doing it might never occur again. It might be objected, of course, that while Parliament was engaged on this important business the colonies would be without civil jurisdiction or trade, and would be subject to military law. What of it?

[65]

The Colonists have lived without Trade, or with that Pittance of Trade which was worse than none, and without civil jurisdiction, or under that kind of one which was infinitely Tyrannical and oppressive, during the Space of two Years and more; Misfortunes brought on themselves by their own Wickedness and Folly. They may therefore certainly live without them a few Months longer in order to obtain the Benefits of lasting Peace & Liberty. Indeed their Situation will be mended under a military Government. They will at least enjoy Protection and be masters of their own Property, Blessings to which they have been, for a long Time, Strangers.

Trade could be carried on under a military government, debts recovered, performance of contracts enforced, and peace preserved.[15]

Here, in a sentence, was Galloway's concept of the "Benefits of lasting Peace & Liberty": protection of property, collection of debts, enforcement of contracts, conduct of trade—the things by which the Old Empire lived, the ends to which its navy and its army and its civil establishment were directed. But what of his concern for those liberties of the individual— the right of trial by jury, the freedom of the press, the freedom of religion? These were rights that were not discussed in the letters to Richard Jackson.

Dartmouth may or may not have communicated Galloway's ideas to Lord North, but at least he indicated to Galloway that he approved of them. His reply, perhaps lost, is reflected in Galloway's elated expression of appreciation on December 3, 1777:

My Lord, Your Favor of the 21st of May, which your Goodness has condescended to honor me with, I did not receive before this Day. It not only demands but ensures my most grateful Acknowledgments. It is, certainly, one of the most flaterring Circumstances of my Life, that the Principles I have adopted and

[15] *Ibid.*, No. 2055; Serle forwarded a copy of this letter to Dartmouth on April 3: "I am just favored by Mr. Galloway with the copy of another letter, which he has dispatched to his old Friend Mr. Jackson, on the present Posture of Affairs"; *Stevens's Facsimiles*, No. 2056.

the Sentiments I have held forth to the public in this critical and interesting Period have met with your Lordship's Approbation.[16]

Here, for the first time in years, Galloway experienced that more than comforting reassurance that the defender of established authority feels when he learns that established authority is in sympathetic hands. Government, he must have reflected, was safe, and the future secure. But he was soon to learn that established authority, sympathetic as it was to loyalties in the mass, could be cruelly indifferent to individual allegiance.

During the succeeding year Galloway plunged wholeheartedly into the problem of assisting in the subjugation of the colonies. In addition to the plan that he had drawn up on the subject of foraging, he submitted to Sir William Howe information about the Middle States and suggested that Philadelphia be approached by way of the Delaware. Much to Galloway's disgust, Howe went by way of Chesapeake Bay, but when he finally occupied Philadelphia, he made Galloway superintendent of civil administration within the city, with command over the police and the port. In addition to his many municipal duties, Galloway found time to accumulate valuable evidence respecting the state of affairs in America and, having opened a correspondence with Lord Dartmouth, he sent many lengthy reports to the Lord Privy Seal about trade, population, public debts, and the disaffected.[17]

Galloway later told Lord George Germain that he had persuaded General Howe to establish a civil police in Philadelphia in order to convince the people that England "meant to do what was right." This establishment, according to Galloway, "gave general satisfaction, because it was es-

[16] *Ibid.*, No. 2069.

[17] Galloway's various letters to Dartmouth and their enclosures of private reports on population, trade, public· debts, etc., are reproduced in *Stevens's Facsimilies,* Nos. 2069, 2070, 2075, 2078, 2079, 2080, 2081, 2082, 2083, 2084, 2085, 2086, 2087, 2090, 2092-2098, 2100. See also, *Hist. MSS Com., Fourteenth Report, Appendix, Part X,* 448, 454, 459, 462, 466, 467.

teemed a prelude to their being soon restored to the Enjoyment of Civil Liberty, and a Settled Constitution between the two Countries." The Proprietary family and officials were not among those who shared this general satisfaction. On December 14, Anne Penn wrote to Lady Juliana Penn that

Mr. Galloway is appointed Superintendent General in the Civil Department here, with very uncommon powers, which I am afraid may affect the Proprietary Interest, as he has always been a great enemy to it, and was at the head of a faction that endeavoured to overturn the Government some years ago. He has given his opinion as a Lawyer that all the estates in America are forfeited by the present Rebellion, & has declared that all Proprietary Governments were inadequate to support the Interests of the Crown. These opinions which are the effects of his prejudices & resentments, may perhaps render him a dangerous person to fill so important a station. It may be necessary therefore for your Ladyship to exert your interest at home to counteract any designs he may have with regard to the Proprietary affairs as soon as possible. I do not suppose that Sr William Howe was acquainted with the real character or Politics of Mr. Galloway when he appointed him to his present Office.[18]

While Anne Penn's fears were unjustified, and while Galloway's administration of the civil authority of the city seems to have been exemplary, he did believe firmly that the proprietary governments should be eliminated from any new imperial constitution. To that extent, and also in her observation upon Sir William Howe's ignorance of Galloway's politics, Anne Penn, as later events revealed, was a woman of very discerning mind. The General called upon her the day after she wrote to Lady Juliana, and doubtless learned what some Philadelphians thought of his Civil Administrator.

But that hard winter's work by Galloway in behalf of government brought bitter disappointment. Late in May—two days after the extravagant *Meschianza* given in honor of Howe—Ambrose recorded

[18] Anne Penn to [Lady Juliana Penn], Dec. 14, 1777; Hist. Soc. of Pa.

a long Conversation with my Friend Mr. G[alloway] respecting affairs, on wch we were rather sad. He mentioned, that all the important Intelligence wch he had procured thro' the Winter for the Genl had not cost Govt. £500; whereas Skinner (according to Col. Innis) had disbursed £12000 upon that account in the Jersies during the former year.[19]

But if such treatment of a loyal American was galling, what Galloway learned the next morning from Samuel Shoe-maker was bitter disillusion. Howe had advised Shoemaker "to make his Peace with the States, who, he supposed, would not treat them [the Loyalists] harshly; for that it was probable, on Account of the French War, the Troops would be withdrawn." This information, Serle noted, "was soon circulated about the Town, & filled all our Friends with melancholy on the Apprehension of being speedily deserted now a Rope was (as it were) about their necks, & all their Property subject to Confiscation. The information chilled me with Horror, and with some Indignation when I reflected upon the miserable Circumstances of the Rebels, &c."[20] The next day Galloway received from Howe and Clinton, through Sir William Erskine, confirmation of this disheartening news.

It filled my poor Friend [wrote Serle] . . . with Horror & melancholy on the View of his deplorable Situation; exposed to the Rage of his bitter Enemies, deprived of a Fortune of about £70,000, and now left to wander like Cain upon the Earth without Home, & without Property. Many others are involved in the like dismal Case for the same Reason—attachment to their King & Country, & opposition to a Set of daring Rebels, who might soon be crushed by spirited Exertions. . . . I endeavoured to console, as well as to advise my Friend. I felt for him & with him. Nothing remains for him but to attempt Reconciliation with (what I may *now* venture to call) *the United States of America*; which probably may not succeed, as they have attainted him in Body & Goods by an Act of the Legislature of Pennsylvania.

[19] Tatum, *op. cit.*, 295.
[20] *Ibid.*, 295.

[69]

Galloway summoned the magistrates of Philadelphia and told them of Howe's advice, "wch filled many an honest & loyal Heart with Grief & Despair."[21]

During that gloomy week-end of May 23-24, 1778, Galloway made a last effort to persuade Sir Henry Clinton not to abandon the leading city and one of the richest provinces to the enemy. In two long conferences on the twenty-fifth "he imparted every Intelligence of this Country in his Power, & much to his Satisfaction." Sir William Erskine, who felt that if Galloway's ideas were followed the Revolution would soon be at an end, also interposed with Clinton. But all this was to no avail: the King himself, under his sign manual, had ordered the evacuation of Philadelphia and the march northward to join Sir Guy Carleton.

Early in June the Carlisle Commissioners arrived, and Galloway, desperately grasping at some source of encouragement, felt that all was not lost. "The Spirits of the Town seemed revived upon the Occasion; People conceiving a Hope, that they shall not now be abandoned." On Sunday evening, June 7, Galloway talked with George Johnstone, one of the Commissioners, on the subject of an imperial constitution. Johnstone suggested that Great Britain should send two representatives to each of the colonial assemblies, and they in turn should send one each to Parliament; that taxation of the colonies should be relinquished, but that Parliament should have supreme legislative power in all other cases; and that this would lay the foundation of what he called a "Foederal Union." Galloway, according to Serle, "represented, in its true light, the absurdity & Impracticability of such a Scheme, and told him that no foederal Union cd subsist but between Independent States, and that to propose it wd be a virtual acknowledgemt. of American Independency."[22] Abandoned by the army whose efforts he believed must prepare the way

[21] *Ibid.*, 295-96.
[22] *Ibid.*, 298*ff.*, 307.

for a new imperial constitution, Galloway felt the humiliating despair of realizing that a peace commissioner who had raised hopes could only talk political nonsense.

In the middle of June, convinced of the uselessness of further effort in America, Galloway departed, for the last time, from the city and province in which he had so been long a powerful and influential figure. Now, stripped of his wealth, attainted of treason by his own countrymen, parted from his wife forever, he turned his thoughts toward that government which had rewarded his loyalty and his hopes with indifference, abandonment, and a pittance of salary for his hard work and information. Late in October 1778 he sailed with his daughter from New York for London.

CHAPTER V

CONSTITUTIONALIST IN EXILE

In 1770, when Galloway had experienced the attacks of Dickinson and Goddard and other political enemies, he had almost decided to retire from public life. As he looked back in exile upon those days, he must have felt that they were, by comparison with what he later suffered, relatively peaceful and secure. His life was now wrecked, and those whom he had looked to with hope and optimism had given him humiliation and neglect. The blow was incomparably greater than any he had ever suffered, but his courage and determination were only strengthened by adversity. Far from weakly yielding, he drove ahead during the next few years with an unrelenting intensity of purpose and a ceaseless energy worthy of a great cause—and of a better hearing than the British government gave him. Almost at once, and with furious indignation, he attacked two of the principal questions in the heart of American affairs: the want of energy and decisiveness in the conduct of the war and the lack of consideration for the plight of the Loyalists. On these heads, his outraged feelings caused him to attack high personages openly and unreservedly. But perhaps closest to his heart was his cherished idea for the formation of a new imperial constitution. On this subject alone, though he continued to press it with undiminished zeal, was he temperate and cool.

Pamphlet after pamphlet dropped from his pen. Sir William Howe was the first to be attacked. In June 1779 Galloway was examined by the Committee on American Papers of the House of Commons, but his testimony against Sir William Howe, according to Israel Mauduit, was adroitly turned by Edmund Burke into an inquisition of Galloway himself.[1]

[1] See Mauduit's marginal comments in the copy of the *Examination* in the Library of Congress. Cf. Mass. Hist. Soc., *Procs.*, XLIV, *passim*.

Galloway felt that the Whig opposition in Parliament was conspiring to prove that the colonies were too strong to be conquered, that their inhabitants were almost totally disaffected to the Crown, and that the forces sent to America to suppress the rebellion were quite inadequate. This, he felt, was only an attempt to muddy the waters so as "to conceal from the public eye the shameful misconduct of the American war, to place to the account of Administration all of the national misfortunes . . . and . . . to demonstrate the disgraceful necessity of suffering two-thirds of the British territory to be dismembered by rebellion from the dominion of the state."[2] To expose this effort, Galloway published *Letters to a Nobleman on the Conduct of the War in the Middle Colonies*, and, not content with attacking "the military indolence and misconduct of men, who have sacrificed to party and faction their own honour, the glory of their Sovereign, and the dignity of the nation," he turned on the admiral, Lord Howe, in *A Letter to the Right Honourable Viscount H—e, on his Naval Conduct in the American War*. Both of these lengthy pamphlets were published in 1779, and in the next year two others came from his pen: *Historical and Political Reflections on the Rise and Progress of the American Rebellion*—which made an attempt to trace the spirit of independence back to the Peace of 1763 and to fasten much of the responsibility for it upon the Presbyterians—and *Cool Thoughts on the Consequences to Great Britain of American Independence*, which painted the future of England in black colors if independence were acknowledged.

America independent! [he exclaimed] the West Indies conquered by France or annexed to America! our fisheries on the banks of *Newfoundland*, and the *American coasts*, with all the trade of the *West Indies* and *America*, cut off from the *British* commerce! where are our nurseries of seamen? . . . Our navy, the *great bulwark of our safety*, will be sunk into contempt, and the *British Flag* will be no more respected in the British seas, than the *lugsail* of an *oyster-boat*![3]

² *Letters to a Nobleman*, "Advertisement" leaf.
³ *Plain Truth* (London, 1780), 5.

[73]

In short, he felt that England would soon lose her own independence. The humiliating sight of French and Spanish squadrons in British seas in 1779 and 1780, the nearly bankrupt state of public finances, the indecisiveness of the North ministry, and the disgrace of the slovenly conduct of the war in America caused many others to share Galloway's alarm. But if the brothers Howe had disgraced themselves, General Burgoyne also had much to answer for—and Galloway drew up, but apparently never published, an attack on him even more savage than his pamphlets on the Howes.[4]

On the plight of the Loyalists in London, Galloway was almost as bitter. Because of his prominence in the colonies, his talents as a lawyer, and his readiness with the pen, he soon established himself as a leader among these unfortunates. In a letter to a member of the ministry on "the great neglect of American gentlemen, now in England, and the fatal consequences which will follow it," Galloway gave warning at the outset that he was "not to expect either flattery, or deception, the two principal ingredients of a tasty address to a King's minister." Ministers, so Galloway affirmed in blunt language, had not viewed the American Loyalists in the proper light, and if justice did not compel him to do so, political exigencies might. These political refugees, Galloway pointed out, were the first characters in their several professions in all of the British provinces; they had sacrificed everything except their loyal principles, and "their demand on government is bottom'd on the strict obligation between government and loyalty, or in other words, on the indissoluble connexion between obedience and protection." Government had not afforded them protection. "Such men have long ago felt the tormenting sting of neglect, and the wound is daily increasing." Could they be expected to risk their lives and property again in support of a government so indifferent

[4] The original manuscript of Galloway's letter to Burgoyne, together with a fair copy of it, is in the Manuscripts Division of the Library of Congress. A microfilm copy of these two documents is in the Princeton University Library.

to their just claims? How could America ever be subdued if these men were to return to their respective provinces and throw their weight in with the enemies of government, armed also with "uncontrovertable arguments your neglectful conduct furnish such spirits with"? Such men would not fail to proclaim to the world their unparalleled sufferings and a neglect that placed them in the same class with "unnoticed vagabonds." Worse, government added insult to its general neglect by selecting for employment and promotion those Loyalists who had been unknown and unnoticed in the colonies, despite the fact that there were in London gentlemen accustomed to "live in a genteel stile, had as good connexions, were as reputably educated, and as much respected" as any in America.[5]

Here, indeed, was the real betrayal. Galloway and his fellow Loyalists—those with connections, those accustomed to wealth and gentility, those used to respect for their position and class—had exiled themselves and sacrificed the material bases of their way of life out of loyalty to a government whose boast was its adherence to the idea of a ruling *élite*. These exiled Americans, Galloway insisted, were entitled to be regarded as a colonial *élite*. But the government which existed by recognizing all gradations of honors and stations apparently had no such concept of the functions of gentility in its overseas territories. "Well informed Americans," Galloway assured the minister,

do not place all happiness in opulence, or splendid shew. Had their souls been bare enough to be directed by such groveling principles, you would not have been troubled with their persons. The danger was obvious to every one who, but slightly, considered the casualties natural to war, the distance between Great Britain and America, and the necessary embarrassments resulting therefrom, the impossibility, under the British Constitution, to

[5] This undated manuscript is in the Library of Congress; it is ascribed to Lord Howe, but this I question.

[75]

apply a remedy as sudden and as efficacious as the disease required, and what was worse than all the other difficulties, the great and essential support which the rebel Americans had, even in the councils of Great Britain. A personal notice is what gentlemen exceedingly value. In this your Lordship has been extremely remiss. And others, whose peculiar duty, even in point of policy, it was to practice it, have also entirely neglected it. This, at least, the exiled Americans, I mean certain classes of them, had a right to expect, and receive. And the omission of it consequently has wounded many of those gentlemen in the most tender part. And I know that the sensations produced thereby are much more severe, and raise a higher degree of resentment, than the mere want of money. Poverty, my Lord, to persons used to affluence is distressing enough, but if, to that calamity, you add neglect of merit, which in fact amounts to utter contempt, the burthen becomes really insufferable.[6]

Neglect of merit amounted to neglect of rank, and that in turn meant repudiation of the concept of an *élite*, a concept that might be taken for granted in London, but one that, in the eyes of some colonials, warranted respect enough to compel large sacrifice. Galloway, feeling this repudiation with such burning indignation, believing that the idea of an *élite* meant more to some men than their property, yet could not understand that other men in America could respond with equal fervor to the concept that all men were born free and equal and that government governed by their free consent. Thus it was that Galloway, Serle, and others, believing other Americans valued the British system of rank and station as they themselves did, so often included in their Plans of Union the provision for an American nobility. A perfect specimen of the British official attitude toward the harassed Tories, who were caught between two fires, is found in a letter from General Charles Grey to Sir Henry Clinton, dated February 28, 1781:

[6] *Ibid.*

It is a reflection upon this or any other country to encourage such a fellow as Galloway in writing and attacking the character of the administration and generals. For God's sake put no confidence in any of those *loyal* Americans near you. Many are spies upon you, sending home what they know will please.[7]

While recognition for the Loyalists in London was never accorded in the degree that it was desired, the British government was liberal in granting compensation for the somewhat exaggerated claims of losses sustained.[8] It also secured, in articles V and VI of the Treaty of Peace of 1783, the promise that Congress would recommend to the states the adoption of conciliatory measures toward the Loyalists. Over three hundred of the leading exiles were placed on the pension lists of the British government, Galloway among them. But he continued to press the Loyalists' claims to just restitution if not to recognition. In 1783 he published his *Observations on the Fifth Article of the Treaty with America* and, in 1788, *The Claim of the American Loyalists Reviewed and Maintained upon Incontrovertible Principles of Law and Justice.* "Few men in the course of a long life settled more business for others than . . . Joseph Galloway," wrote his daughter some years after his death, "and perhaps seldom anyone gave so much advice gratis. His morning room for twenty years was often crowded, and seldom empty of Americans who received from him his best services in their own affairs."[9] When the British Commission for Enquiring into the Loyalist Claims heard his own case, the board concluded that, despite the fact that he had been a member of Congress, "they are of opinion that during that time he endeavored to promote the constitutional dependence of the colonies on Great Britain—that he has since conducted himself as a zealous loyalist and rendered services to the British Government."[10]

[7] Clinton Papers, William L. Clements Library.
[8] C. H. Van Tyne, *The Loyalists in the American Revolution* (New York, 1902), 243*ff.*
[9] Baldwin, *op. cit.,* XXVI. 438.
[10] *Ibid.*

Of the three hundred and three Loyalists pensioned by the government, only eighteen received sums higher than £200 per annum. Galloway received £500—almost as much as that granted to Governor Robert Eden of Maryland, brother of an under secretary of state. This almost amounted to recognition of his standing.[11]

But during these years of bitter partisanship, Galloway was not merely a controversial pamphleteer plunging into the quarrels of English Whigs and Tories over the conduct of the war, not merely an advocate of recognition and compensation for his fellow Loyalists. In pursuing his favorite plan of establishing an imperial constitution and of drawing the colonies and the realm into closer union, he exhibited some of the elements of disinterested statesmanship. His writings on this subject were devoid of those angry expressions or blunt charges of incompetence or worse which characterized his pamphleteering. He could attack the Dean of Gloucester ferociously for suggesting that England would be better off without the colonies, but he approached the problem of constructing a new imperial organization as dispassionately and as learnedly as the great writers on government from whom he drew his precepts—Locke, Grotius, Burlamaqui, and Puffendorf. He had been driven out of America and he had suffered comparative neglect in England, but he still believed in the greatness of England and in the future greatness of America, and it took almost ten years of disappointed effort to cause him to relinquish the hope that they might still be incorporated in one imperial union.

There were other writers in England at this time, forced at last to think in terms of rebuilding the empire and not in terms of making temporary concessions, who sought to draw up the specifications for the new structure of empire.[12] William Pulteney's *Thoughts on the Present State of Affairs with*

[11] Van Tyne, *op. cit.*, 255.
[12] See Charles F. Mullett's excellent "English Imperial Thinking," *Pol. Sci. Quar.*, XLV. 548-79, for a discussion of these authors.

America and the Means of Conciliation proposed what amounted to home rule for the colonies. An anonymous radical of 1778, in a *Proposal for a Plan toward Reconciliation and Reunion with the Thirteen Provinces in America, and for a Union with the Other Colonies,* advocated complete local autonomy for colonies linked together, not by the Crown, but by an administrative Great Council of State. A yet more radical author, likewise concealed in anonymity, drew up in 1780 a rough plan of an imperial commonwealth, *A Plan on Articles of Perpetual Union, Commerce, and Friendship between Great Britain and her Colonies,* which had much in common with Galloway's ideas on the subject. John Fenton Cawthorne is credited with having written in 1782 another set of plans for the new empire in *A Plan of Reconciliation with America: consistent with the dignity and interests of both countries.* This plan rejected the idea of colonial representation in Parliament and advocated an "American Parliament, whose powers shall resemble those of the Parliaments in Ireland and Great Britain." A plan similar to this, *The Alarm, or a Plan of Pacification with America,* appeared in New York in 1780, but was obviously written by an Englishman. Perhaps the most interesting example of this sort of imperial thinking, and certainly the one with the most bizarre mode of publication, was the one that was thrown into a grate of Benjamin Franklin's residence at Passy.

This rather indirect approach was made by an Englishman who went under the alias Charles de Weissenstein. Franklin told John Adams that "there were in the letter infallible marks, by which he knew that it came from the King [of England], and that it could not have come from any other, without the King's knowledge. What these marks [Adams said] were he never explained to me."[13] The letter, consisting of six closely written folio pages, suggested that Franklin should make known directly to George III the terms on which America would negotiate for peace. It was accom-

[13] C. F. Adams, ed., *Works of John Adams,* III. 177-79.

panied by a "Project for Allaying the present ferments in North America" and by a "Great Outline of the Future Government in North America." The latter provided that "A Great & Solemn Compact shall pass The British Parliament & be registered in the Archives of every State of America. It shall be declared to be Perpetual & irrevokeable but by the free & mutual Consent of both Countries & shall be declared to be the condition of Protection, submission & Union." Each province, having chosen its own form of government, would be protected against any alteration or infringement "by any other Power or pretended Authority whatsoever" except by the free consent of its own legislature. Each province would nominate its own executive officers and all others holding posts of trust, but no American could hold such an office in Great Britain without a special Act of Parliament." A Supreme Court of Universal Jurisdiction over all others throughout the Continent" would be formed, and its judgments would be final except that appeal might lie to the British House of Lords, the supreme court of the empire. Members of the American court, not exceeding two hundred, would hold office for life and would bear titles as Peers of America. A general Congress would assemble once every seven years, or oftener if the King should convene it. Its duty would be to fix the proportion to be paid by every state into the general fund, and its proceedings would be transmitted to Parliament for ratification. A general schedule of import and export duties would be fixed and not changed except by the mutual consent of Parliament and the colony involved. British manufacturers should always have the preference over those of other nations, and no new taxes should be imposed upon them without the consent of Parliament. American ships could sail "at their own Choice to any & every Part of the World, provided they clear out fairly at the Port from whence they sail & at their return do the same." On these terms,

The Laws & Territory of each State & the Persons & commerce of its subjects, shall be guaranteed, defended, & avenged against all enemies whatsoever, by the Whole force of the British Empire. . . . & Great Britain & America shall mutually aid & comfort each other for ever nor shall The King nor the British Parliament assume the authority ever to make Laws for or tax America other than according to this Compact.[14]

Franklin, believing this strange document to come from the King or the ministry, replied as if he expected his letter to be carried to British officials:

We have never asked . . . [independence] of you, we only tell you, that you can have no treaty with us but as an independent state; and you may please yourselves and your children with the rattle of your right to govern us, as long as you have done with that of your King's being King of France, without giving us the least concern, if you do not attempt to exercise it. That this pretended right is indisputable, as you say, we utterly deny. Your Parliament never had a right to govern us, and your King has forfeited it by his bloody tyranny. But I thank you for letting me know . . . that, even if the Parliament should acknowledge our independency, the act would not be binding to posterity, and that your nation would resume and prosecute the claim as soon as they found it convenient from the influence of your passions, and your present malice against us. We suspected before, that you would not be actually bound by your conciliatory acts, longer than till they had served their purpose of inducing us to disband our forces; but we were not certain, that you were knaves by principle, and that we ought not to have the least confidence in your offers, promises, or treaties, though confirmed by Parliament. . . . This proposition of delivering ourselves, bound and gagged, ready for hanging, without even a right to complain, and without a friend to be found afterwards among all mankind, you would have us embrace upon the faith of an act of Parliament! Good God! an act of Parliament! This demonstrates that you do not yet know us, and that you fancy we do not know you.[15]

[14] These documents, together with the letter dated June 13, 1778, are in *Stevens's Facsimiles*, Nos. 835, 836, 837.

[15] Smyth, ed., *Writings of Franklin*, VII. 166-72.

Aside from this indignant refusal to consider such overtures, Franklin's only reply to de Weissenstein was to communicate the documents to Vergennes.

Thus Galloway's writings on the subject of an imperial constitution were but a part of the general background of suggestions being thrown out futilely by English writers at a time when all possibility of liberal imperialism was rapidly fading. Of all those who thought they had the answer to the ministry's problem of colonial administration, none was possessed of more exact information about America than Galloway, none had given up more for the sake of the imperial connection, and none was more persistent in pressing plan after plan upon the attention of the King's ministers. But despite Galloway's superior knowledge of America, his plans savored of the cloistered study and of the dicta of the classical writers on government. Their air of unreality and their obvious appearance of having been produced *in vacuo* did not set them apart from similar writings of English imperialists, even though their author had a vast superiority in experience and knowledge of America. Because they overlooked or misunderstood the real nature of the American Revolution, Galloway's Plans of Union were almost as divorced from the realities of American conditions, or of British politics, as John Locke's Fundamental Constitutions, drawn up for the Lords Proprietors of Carolina a century earlier. The fundamental weakness of Galloway's Plans of Union was that, far from understanding the liberal movement underlying the American Revolution and trying to adapt an imperial constitution to the directions of that movement, they were designed to counteract it. They were *against* any leveling or republican manifestations in the colonies; they were *against* anything that challenged the established institutions of the British structure of government. For this reason, slight as was their chance of serious consideration in England, they could be accepted in America only if they were imposed upon conquered provinces stripped of the opportunity of choice. This much, at least, Galloway clearly realized, and the realization goes far to explain the savage nature of his attacks upon the Howe brothers and upon Burgoyne.

If Galloway possessed a background of exact information about America, the inferences that he drew from it were colored by his harsh experiences and his conservative abhorrence of what the Revolutionary leaders were doing to America and to the empire. Within a month of his arrival in London in 1778, he was in touch with influential persons in the government and was supplying documentary information. Lord Dartmouth, Lord Hardwicke, Thomas Hutchinson, John Robinson, Charles Jenkinson, and others received him and listened to his impassioned pleas. Early in December George III received the following communication from John Robinson, Secretary to the Treasury:

Mr. Robinson has the Honour to transmit for your Majesty's perusal some papers which he has this Day received from Mr. Galway, late Speaker of the late legal Assembly of Pennsylvania, and a warm friend of this Country, who has lately arrived from America, and has lost his all in the Service of this Country. Mr. Robinson presumed to think it might not be disagreeable to your Majesty to be informed of the Sentiments of such a person, and therefore Mr. Robinson has ventured to send the papers, and anxiously hopes he shall not have done amiss.[16]

These papers apparently consisted of a statement of the American debt, a "Proposal for Covering and Reducing the Country as the British Army shall pass through it," and "A State of the Circumstances of Philadelphia when Sir William Howe took Possession of it." The last was the census taken by Galloway of Philadelphia, showing that of the 6,057 houses in the city at that time, only 597 had been "deserted by the disaffected" patriots. Lord Amherst examined this document and reported to the King that he thought it "very exact as to the Houses, Inhabitants, the well affected and the ill affected." Because nine-tenths of the people of Phila-

[16] Fortescue, op. cit., IV. 230, 244, 245-47.

delphia were loyal to the Crown, Galloway reasoned that the same was true of all America, though he later reduced his estimate to four-fifths. Two weeks after Galloway had sent his first documents to the King, he furnished copies of them— presumably at the request of George III—for Lord North, and at the same time he transmitted to the King, through Robinson, two additional papers.[17] It was not, presumably, until 1782, when the North ministry had fallen and Shelburne was in power, that the King expressed in writing an opinion of this prolific American Loyalist. On the morning of June 22, 1782, Shelburne wrote to the King: "I have the honor to send you the most interesting of Mr. Galloway's Papers," and that afternoon the King replied: "The Papers received from Mr. Galloway are certainly very curious; He seems to be an active man and it may not be unwise for Lord Shelburne to show him some civility; time alone can decide whether it would be right it should proceed to anything further."[18] It is not known whether any of the documents that Galloway so assiduously brought to the attention of the King's ministers included his various Plans of Union.

On March 18, 1779, the Representatives of the Freemen of the Commonwealth of Pennsylvania, in session at the State House in Philadelphia, resolved that it was "suitable and necessary that a proper house be provided by the public for the residence of his excellency the president of the supreme executive council of the state for the time being."[19] There was a suitably elegant home one square northward from the State House, on the southeast corner of High and Sixth Streets. It had belonged to one who had been attainted of treason in body and goods, and it was therefore appropriated by statute as the executive residence of George Bryan, radical leader of Pennsylvania's democracy and long-time foe of Joseph Gallo-

[17] *Ibid.*, IV. 236.
[18] *Ibid.*, VI. 64.
[19] *Statutes at Large of Pennsylvania*, IX.

way, who had been its owner and whose wife, now residing there, was forcibly dispossessed.[20]

On that same day, in London, Joseph Galloway addressed to Lord George Germain the first of his various Plans of Union written in exile. In a lengthy covering letter, he explained to Germain the reasons that had led him to "throw together the Hints or Plans of an Union between G[reat] B[ritain] and her Colonies." He believed that the American people,

. . . or a very great majority of them, who are desirous of an Union between the two Countries, are dayly expecting that some System of Polity will be proposed to them by Parliament, in which shall be ascertained the *measure of Civil Power* which is to be in future exercised over them and the *degree of civil Liberty* they are to enjoy, including particularly the Mode by which they shall be enabled to grant to the Crown at all times, their just and *reasonable Proportion of Aids.*

For the Americans had never denied that they should bear their just proportion of the cost of national defense, but in all of their petitions and declarations had explicitly denied the authority and right of Parliament to tax them, and had asserted their willingness to contribute by the levies of their own assemblies to the burden of defense.

Worn down as the People of America are at present [continued Galloway] by Congressional Tyranny and the Distress of three Years ruinous War, they will cheerfully embrace any reasonable Propositions that shall be made to them for the above purposes, which before, when the Spirit of Enthusiasm and Delusion prevailed they would perhaps have rejected with contempt. Indeed this seems to be the *critical Period pointed out by all circumstances* for effecting so important a work. I mean that such a System of Government for the Colonies should be now perfectly digested, and prepared ready to be handed out to every Colony *as soon* as it is reduced to his Majesty's Peace.

[20] See the diary of Grace Growden Galloway, *Penn. Mag. of Hist. and Biog.*, LV. (1931), 32-94.

[85]

Furthermore, as soon as a colony was conquered, its rebel rulers driven out, and all remains of the new state government destroyed, it would

> . . . in respect to Government become a Chart Blanch. Their old form [of government] being given up and totally effaced *by the People themselves*, and the new by the Power of the British Arms, Nothing will remain to be considered but the Proposals made by Government. And the minds of the People having in some Measure lost their Ideas of the Old, and possessing a lively sense of the Oppression of the New, will prevent their recurring back to either.

One colony, Galloway pointed out, had already been reduced and others would in all probability soon follow. Should they be governed by military law and held by armed forces? Much had happened in the two years since Galloway had pointed out to Richard Jackson that such an expedient would be acceptable and even desirable: England was now engaged in a continental war and was threatened with invasion. He now felt that military government would "disgust the minds of the People and make them very restless Subjects," and as for enforcing such a government with the presence of an army, there would not be enough British forces to spare for that purpose. Civil government of some kind must therefore be established *"to preserve the Peace*, to *punish the Factious and seditious*, and *to form a System of Military Defense within itself*, so as to spare the British Force for other Services." If so, were the old forms of government to be reestablished?

> This may be done with some degree of Safety in the Royal Governments. But in those held by Charter it must be attended with the greatest insecurity and Danger. The Governors of some of them are violent Independent Rebels, and all of them save one, have taken the Oath of Allegiance to the New States, and abjured forever the Crown of Britain. Should one of these be reduced—suppose Connecticut or Rhode Island—Is the Governor who has thus abjured his Allegiance to be trusted? Or are the

People in their present Disaffected State to be permitted to elect a New one under their Charter, who have also abjured the Crown of G. Britain? Ought such a character to be trusted, to take upon himself the Administration of the Laws and the Defense of the Colony?

These problems of reconstruction indicated to Galloway the urgent need of holding out to the people "some System of well digested Polity" as soon as the colonies were conquered.

Such a system, he argued, ought in all of its principles to aim at a perfect and perpetual union between the two countries, not at temporary expedients to remedy present conditions.

It should give the People Freedom. This will make them contented under it, but at the same time it should hold up and maintain a sufficient Degree of Power and Authority over them, to preserve the Peace and Order of Society, founded as near as possible *upon those Principles of Policy, upon which the Constitution of the Principal State is founded.*

This would preserve the same balance of power in both countries.

But above all things, [Galloway insisted] the Prerogatives of the Crown in their full Extent should be extended and preserved inviolate, and every *principle of Democracy* and *Aristocracy*, interfering with them, to be found in the old Forms of the Colonial Governments should be carefully avoided; because it is to them principally, that all the Seditions in America, and the present Rebellion in particular owe their Origin. And because where they exist to the Prejudice and Diminution of the Royal Prerogatives, the Execution of the Laws have been relaxed and the Reigns of Government ever held with a feeble Hand.

What Galloway had in mind when he spoke of principles of aristocracy in the colonial governments was not such as prevailed in the government of Great Britain, of which he

[87]

approved, but the presence of the proprietary governments of Lord Baltimore and the Penn family.

Such a system, he thought, would not only be acceptable to America but would be cheerfully embraced. It was natural for a people

. . . in the possession of every Blessing that civil Polity can bestow, and having incurred the resentment of a powerful Nation, who are on the Verge of bringing them back to their Duty, to enquire what is to be their fate. I therefore found before I left Pennsylvania and came over to G. Howe, that all the well Disposed People, wished for *some just and definitive Propositions from G. Britain.* When I came to New York the same Desire prevailed, and when I returned to Philadelphia, the numerous Inhabitants who remained there, almost unanimously concur'd in their applications to me, to know whether they were to be Governed by military Law, or restored to their Civil Rights, and still wishing that the wisdom of Parliament, would propose some System of Government, under which, the causes of the present Dispute should be removed. To convince them that G. Britain meant to do what was right, I prevailed on the General to establish a Civil Police in that City. It gave general satisfaction, because it was esteemed a prelude to their being soon restored to the Enjoyment of Civil Liberty, and a Settled Constitution between the two Countries.

Galloway believed that if such an imperial constitution had been drawn up by Parliament and had accompanied the display of armed force from the beginning, "It would have satisfied the Friends of the Crown, carried conviction to the Minds of the Men of Sense, and prevented even the Credulous and more ignorant part of the People from believing what the determined enemies to Government persuaded them to believe—That the Parliament intended to enslave them." Even now, he urged, such a step would remove fears and jealousies from the minds of the people and would "tend more than anything else to distract the Councils of the Congress, create Divisions among the People, and in all Probability, be equally Effectual with the Power of Arms in Suppressing the Rebellion and finally restoring the Peace of both Countries." The terms of accommodation previously held out to the Americans, he believed, had been too indecisive. But most of all they had "wanted those political principles which are absolutely necessary to the Establishment of a Permanent Union" and had aimed at temporary expedients rather than permanency.[21] For these reasons Galloway submitted to Germain alternative Plans of Union based upon such principles.

The first of these Plans provided for "a Representation of Parliament as in the cases of Chester, Durham, Wales and Scotland."[22] Though much of Galloway's imperial thinking was divorced from reality, this proposal of colonial representation in Parliament was so much so that even he admitted its impracticability. Nevertheless he submitted it because his reading of Locke and other classical writers on government had given him a few basic principles that he could not relinquish: as distinguished from a mere multitude of people, the state was a body politic having a single supreme will or sovereignty; the inferior members or parts of a state should be governed by those same principles with which the state itself is governed; the subordinate members or parts are bound to yield obedience to the supreme will and authority of the state; and this supreme will is the legislative authority. Unity in legislation, therefore, should be sought after in any Plan of Union because it would bind and cement the members of society, would collect and command the power of defense and of internal order, and it would promote and establish "that similarity of Laws, Regulations and policy, which is necessary to create the sameness of Customs, Habits and Manners, among the people, which fixes the national attachment and the Harmony and uniformity of sentiments, that induce them to Act as one Body in all Matters where

[21] Galloway to Germain, March 18, 1779; Stopford-Sackville MSS, William L. Clements Library.
[22] *Ibid.*, see below, Appendix II.

their common welfare is concerned." Two supreme and independent powers in a single society were "utterly inadvisable and absurd" by any principles of polity or even by natural law. But a separation of legislative powers would be symbolic of separation into two or more sovereign societies. Galloway appealed to the experience with Scotland, Wales, Chester, and Durham and to the history of the Roman empire to prove that the unitary type of government was the most effective of all. Indeed, "This unity in Legislature is most perfect in absolute monarchy . . . and could mankind be certain of always Placing on the Throne a prince of Wisdom and Goodness reason would certainly instruct them to prefer it . . . to all other Forms."

But if representation in Parliament was objected to by Great Britain or by America, then Galloway would urge as his second form of government for the empire an "American Branch of the British Legislature . . . established in America" and consisting of a representative appointed by the Crown, an upper house likewise appointed, and a representation of the people to be chosen by the assemblies of the several colonies. The upper branch of the legislature, corresponding to the House of Lords in England, were to hold their offices during life and to be "vested with some degree of Rank and Dignity above the Commons." Thus the aristocratic principle would be transferred to the colonies. This American counterpart of the Parliament at Westminster differed, therefore, from the American legislature that Galloway had proposed in his Plan of Union of 1774, which consisted only of a representative of the Crown and of a Grand Council representative of the people. But in both Plans, indeed in almost identical language, it was stipulated that the American legislature was to be an inferior branch of Parliament, its jurisdiction was to extend, in both civil and criminal matters, to affairs of general concern to all or more than one of the colonies, and, most important of all, legislation might be originated either in England or in America, but would require the assent of both Parliament and the American branch to become law.

In its broad outline, therefore, this Plan of 1779 was the same as that of 1774 with the addition of a second chamber and of the aristocratic principle. Galloway felt that it was necessary to introduce such an aristocratic principle in the American branch in order to give to the Crown weight and influence and tò preserve "the same Ballance of Power, between the Crown and the people in America, as in Great Britain." Democracy without the checks and balances of aristocracy and monarchy would be dangerous to the state. Stripped of its abstractions, what Galloway really meant by forming a subordinate legislature on the same principles as that of the parent state was that he regarded the British constitution, with its monarchic and aristocratic features, as worthy of being preserved and emulated. He insisted, of course, that the principle should apply whether the parent body was a monarchy, an aristocracy, a democracy, or a mixture of the three. These forms of government, "being opponent in their Social Natures to each other . . . are mixed together to check each other's excess and to form a Just Ballance."

Aside from this difference in the form and character of the American legislature, the Plan of Union of 1779 differed in other important respects from that of 1774. First of all, the prerogative of the Crown was given more protection; whereas by the Plan of 1774 the right of calling, proroguing, or adjourning the Grand Council was vested in that body and the President General, by the Plan of 1779 this right was reserved to the Crown. The appointment of all colonial governors, judicial, ministerial, and executive officers, treasurers, sheriffs, coroners, collectors of revenue, etc., was also vested in the Crown. In the Continental Congress of 1774, one of the principal arguments advanced in favor of the Plan that Galloway submitted to that body was that it left the existing forms of colonial government untouched. But in 1779 Galloway was convinced that "the prevalence of the Aristocratical as well as Democratical principles of the proprietary and Charter Governments in America has formed the Great Source from whence the present Rebellion has Sprung." For this reason his Plan of Union of 1779 provided that all of the colonies should be reduced to the uniform status of royal provinces. Had that been done in the beginning, he declared, "America had not known a Rebellion."

Would the Americans accept a Plan of Union which changed their institutions so radically when, in 1774, they had scornfully rejected one that protected their general interests without such interference in their local governments? Galloway admitted that, in view of the state of political parties in America, it would be good policy to propose that form of imperial constitution which would be most agreeable to the people. But, while pointing out to Germain that "many men of the best understanding, weight, and influence in the Colonies" wished his Plan of 1774 had been adopted, he did not indicate the radical differences between the two Plans, nor the fact that the absence from the former of some of the provisions of the latter had been one of its most appealing features with "men of the best understanding."

Lord George Germain had been publicly disgraced and removed from the Privy Council for his behavior at the Battle of Minden, but now, as commissioner for trade and plantations, as secretary of state for the colonies, as one of the chief pillars of support in the North ministry, was just the minister whom Galloway might have expected to approve his radical Plan of Union.[23] Germain, an intimate friend of such conservatives as Mansfield and Wedderburn, had held firmly to the belief that the Americans should be compelled by force to recognize the sovereignty of Parliament before offers of conciliation were made to them. This had been his position when, in 1776, the Howe brothers were authorized to nego-

[23] George H. Guttridge, "Lord George Germain in Office, 1775-1782," Am. Hist. Rev., XXXIII. 23-43.

tiate with the Americans—a position that he had stoutly defended against the less forceful North and Dartmouth. But much had happened to the realm and to Germain since 1776. Saratoga and the abortive campaign of 1777 had affected him deeply. Early in 1778 his wife had died, and for a time he retired from public life, convinced that "A man at my time of life, depress'd by misfortunes, will make but a bad figure in an office that requires full vigor of mind, activity and diligence."[24] On the heel of these adversities came the Franco-American alliance. Germain did resume the duties of his office, but wearily and without his former vigor. At one time or another, he was on bad terms with all of his commanders in America—the Howe brothers, Carleton, Burgoyne, Clinton—but he did have influence with the King and with Lord North. However, in addition to being depressed by misfortunes, Germain in 1779 was fully occupied with the primary assumption on which Galloway's Plan of Union was based—the problem of trying to conquer the colonies—and he needed no reminder of that fact. If he laid the Plan before the King or Lord North, or even if he acknowledged it to Galloway, the evidence of it has apparently not survived.[25]

The Plan itself nevertheless survived in a curious way. During the time that he had spent with the British forces under Howe and Clinton, Galloway had probably met one Major John Morrison of Newport, Deputy Quartermaster General. Possibly their meeting came about through Ambrose Serle, who in December, 1777, was with Lord Howe at Newport, dined at Morrison's home, listened at some length to the importunate conversation of Morrison's father-in-law, Joseph Wanton, Jr., and, irritated by what he considered the vulgarity of democratic Newport, agreed heartily with Mrs. Morrison's grandfather, Governor Joseph Wanton,

[24] *Ibid.*, XXXIII. 31.

[25] Galloway is said to have appeared as a witness against General Howe at the suggestion of Germain; George A. Ward, ed., *Journal and Letters of the Late Samuel Curwen* (New York, 1842), 527.

that the Americans "would not rest, till they had overthrown everything that stood in the way of their favorite objects, *Republicanism & Presbyterianism.*"[26] At any rate, it seems apparent that some time during the year 1777 or 1778 Galloway and Morrison met and exchanged ideas about an imperial constitution.

For, at Greenwich on November 15, 1779, Morrison addressed a letter to Sir Henry Clinton which began as follows: "May it please your Excellency, the enclosed is a Copy of a Plan, which I would humbly propose to your Excellency's consideration, and if it meets with your Excellency's approbation, I would with your Permission, seize the first opportunity of going to Europe to lay it before My Lords, North & Germaine, and I should not make the least doubt, if carry'd into execution, under your Excellency's Auspices, but, that America would be conquered this Insuing Campaign."

"The enclosed" was "A Plan for facilitating the Reduction of his Majesty's revolved Colonies, and for afterwards retain-

[26] Lorenzo Sabine, in his *American Loyalists*, p. 476, gives a sketch of a New Hampshire minister named John Morrison who was ordained in Peterborough in 1766, served in the American army in Cambridge until the battle of Bunker Hill, entered the commissary department of the British army, and died in Charleston, South Carolina, in 1782. It is evident from this sketch that Sabine has confused two persons of the same name. The Major John Morrison who interested himself with Galloway in their Plans of Union was British, not American, as is evident from his letter to Sir Henry Clinton, Nov. 15, 1779: "As I have had the honour of Commanding a Brigade of Seapoys, in the service of the East India Company (consisting between 4 and 5 thousand men) with honour to myself and satisfaction to my employers; I hope your Excellency will approve of, (especially as my better half is American) my soliciting a Command in the Corps of Loyal Refugees"; ms. in the Clinton Papers, The William L. Clements Library. In April, 1778, Morrison was stationed at Rhode Island as Deputy Quartermaster General; letter to Sir Henry Clinton, April 2, 1778, *ibid. A List of the General and Staff Officers and of the Officers in the Several British . . . Regiments serving in North-America under . . . Sir Henry Clinton* (New York, 1779), p. 5, lists John Morrison as Deputy Commissary General, and a similar manuscript list in the Clements Library, dated October 16, 1781, and corrected to May 10, 1782, shows Morrison holding the same office at Charleston, South Carolina. That this Major John Morrison did not die in 1782, as Sabine states, is indicated by the fact that he presented one of the Plans of Union to Henry Dundas in 1788. *Cf.* Tatum, ed., *Journal of Ambrose Serle*, 271, 272, 273.

ing them in a proper Subordination to the Parent State; humbly proposed to his Excellency Sir Henry Clinton, Commander in Chief &c. &c. &c." This Plan, of which Morrison was probably the sole author, was brief but explicit:[27]

"The Refugees to be imbodyed, and to act under such officers as they shall appoint; and that your Excellency would be pleased to grant them power, to act in such manner as they shall think proper, to promote his Majesty's Service. To receive Pay as his Majesty's Other forces, whilst they are imbody'd, To be reimbursed by their Respective Provinces, out of the Estates of the Rebels, for all damages they have sustained by their Rebellious Brethren, which damages they shall prove on Oath, before a Committee of their Neighbours, appointed for that purpose, before the supreme Judge, or Justice, of the Province.

"As soon as a Province, or part of it, is Reduced to his Majesty's Obedience, the Civil Law, and the following form of Government, with your Excellency's permission, is immediately to take place. Each Province, to have a Lord Lieutenant appointed by the King, with a fixed Salary, paid by the Province.

"The King to give blank Patents, to be filled up by your Excellency, for Creating six Barons, for the small, and twelve for the large Provinces, which are to be formed into houses of Lords, The Commons to be Chosen as usual but to continue for three years.

"A General Parliament to meet every year, composed of one half of the Barons from each Province, and of the Commons from each Provincial Parliament in proportion to the number of Barons as four to one.

"Your Excellency, as Viceroy, to represent the King, with such an appointment, as the Crown shall think fit, for the Dignity of the King's Representative, which is to be paid by

[27] The letter and the Plan are in the Clinton Papers, The William L. Clements Library.

the Provinces; this Parliament to determine on the number of Troops necessary for the defence of the Country, which are to be paid by America; and to maintain, a certain number of men of War as shall be agreed on; The proportions of which expences, which settled by the General Parliament, are to be raised by the Provincial Parliaments, in such manner as they shall Judge most expedient: That no Taxes shall be levied from America, by the Parliament of Great Britain, nor its Trade laid under any other restrictions, but the Enumerated articles; Rice only excepted, and that all Wines may be imported into America, without first landing in England.

"The Viceroy to Appoint all Crown Officers, excepting the Lord Lieutenants, the Lord Lieutenants to have power to appoint all Provincial officers; The Judges to be appointed for Life, with a Salary of Four Hundred per annum; The Clergy of the Church of England, to have fixed Salaries of two hundred per annum with a house in Towns, in the Country at one hundred with a house and Glebe worth thirty Pounds a year; In the Capitals of the large Provinces, they may be allowed three Hundred. All Dissenting Clergymen to have one hundred a year in Towns, and in the Country, Fifty, with a house and small Glebe."

Ten days later, November 25, 1779, Morrison addressed another letter to Sir Henry Clinton: "As I have obtained your Excellency's permission, and that of the Commissary General, to go to England by the first Convoy, I should be extremely happy, if your Excellency would approve of my laying the Plan . . . before my Lords North, and Germaine, and I will not make the least doubt, if it meets your Excellency's approbation, that the year 1780, will hail your Excellency, Conqueror and Viceroy of North America."[28]

Again Clinton apparently gave his consent, for Morrison arrived in England early in 1780 and presented to Lord George Germain a plan almost identical with that laid before Clinton the preceding November. Galloway may have as-

[28] *Ibid.*

sisted Morrison in making some minor changes in the document, such as reducing the number of barons in the large provinces from twelve to ten, providing for salaries of £400 for judges and £600 for chief judges, and suggesting that "A Bishop at New York with an appointment of fifteen hundred or two thousand per Annum would be of the utmost service to Great Britain." Germain evidently replied to Morrison about this Plan of Union, but his reply exists only in the endorsement on the document and is so cryptic as to conceal effectively any opinion that Germain may have had: "My dear Morrison you mistake the date July for November."[29]

This Plan of Union states categorically that it was "proposed by Major John Morrison" to Lord George Germain. Morrison later said that he had joined with Galloway in March, 1780, in presenting a Plan of Union to Germain and this doubtless refers to a seven-page document, similarly titled, which is also to be found among the Germain papers. This document, in effect, combined the Plan that Galloway had sent to Germain on March 18, 1779, with the much briefer Plan submitted by Morrison. It embraced all of the important features of the Galloway Plan without presenting the arguments that went with the earlier document. It was undoubtedly the result of a collaboration between Galloway and Morrison, with Galloway furnishing most of the ideas on government that were incorporated in it and Morrison supplying those provisions designed to recruit the Loyalist forces and reduce the colonies in a military sense.

This joint Plan of Union followed its predecessors in offering the alternative proposal of colonial representation in Parliament. In order to facilitate the reduction of the colonies, three commissioners were to be appointed, one "of the Military profession, and two well acquainted with the principles of the British Constitution." Their duties were to seize the

[29] This three-page Plan, bearing Germain's endorsement, is in the Stopford-Sackville Manuscripts in The William L. Clements Library.

disaffected, collect and arm the Loyalists, and direct the taking of oaths of allegiance. A proclamation of general pardon was to be issued and at the same time the terms of the Plan of Union were to be made public. The structure of this imperial government was the same as that of the Galloway Plan of 1779: a Lord Lieutenant and an upper house appointed by the Crown and a lower house elected by the colonial assemblies. But the Galloway-Morrison Plan provided that the general statutes of the realm and the common law should be declared in force in America, a bishop of the Anglican Church should be established in America, and, while liberty of conscience should be tolerated,

All General Ecclesiastical Committees, Assemblies and Synods, consisting of the Members of more Society's or Congregations than One, and All standing Conventions, Committees, Town Meetings and Associations not authorised by any Law, be declared unlawful and Siditious Assemblies and punishable by Fine, and Imprisonment.[30]

As if to make this startling invasion of civil liberties seem less rigorous, Galloway and Morrison suggested that an occasional meeting for the purpose of petitioning against grievances should not be considered an unlawful assembly. The Plan also contained radical departures in respect of trade and navigation, but since Galloway argued these provisions more fully in a subsequent Plan of Union, they will be discussed below.

The collaboration with Galloway inspired Morrison to continue his efforts in the direction of an imperial union. He returned to America and while stationed at Charleston in the summer of 1782, wrote to Charles James Fox, who was Secre-

[30] Stopford-Sackville Manuscripts, The William L. Clements Library. This document is in Galloway's handwriting. Except for the fact that this Plan of Union of 1780 proposed (1) colonial representation in Parliament as an alternative, (2) provided for one American bishop instead of two, and (3) did not contain the section dividing American colonies into three districts, it was substantially the same as that submitted by Morrison to Dundas in 1788; see Appendix 5.

tary of State for the Southern Department, and proposed to raise ten thousand slaves, at no cost to government, in order to reduce the Southern provinces.

If Administration would not wish to appear in it at present, [he added] let me be supported secretly with money, Arms, and Clothing; and I will suffer the Severest Torture that ever was Inflicted on man, if I do not bring about a Reconciliation, on the most Honorable Terms to both Countries in six months after I receive approbation from Administration.[31]

Such zeal, especially after Yorktown, must have been welcomed by the long-suffering Loyalists with whom Morrison had talked in London. And it no doubt explains why Galloway became associated with him. Morrison also advanced another suggestion to Fox. If government did not approve the raising of slaves to form an army, he would

. . . endeavor to divide the People of this Country, by setting up a Third Interest, by Collecting all those who are willing to be connected with Great Britain, on the following Plan of Government: the Two Floridas, Georgia and the two Carolinas, to form one large Government, and to be Governed by a Lord Lieutenant, to have two Houses of Parliament, but that they should be a Branch of the British Legislature. That is to say, no Law should be Valid, before it had past the British and American Houses of Parliament. If a Law was moved for, in the British Parliament, and had gone through the Necessary Forms, it could not pass into a Law till it had mett the approbation of the American Branch, and in the same manner a Law might be agitated in the American Parliament but cannot Pass into a Law till it has the sanction of the British Parliament. . . . My Plan would take in all the Present Friends of Government, and two thirds of those who are now against us.

In short, Morrison was outlining to Fox the Plan of Union which Galloway had submitted to Germain in 1779, and was suggesting that it be put into operation in the Southern provinces. Morrison further informed Fox that he had arrived

[31] Copy in MSS Division, Library of Congress; dated at Charleston, S. C., July 10, 1782.

in London in 1780 and had "laid before my Lord George Germain a Plan similar to the above" and had also given a copy of it to General Leslie. Even so late as March 7, 1788, Morrison sent to Henry Dundas a copy of "A Plan for facilitating the reduction of the Revolted Colonies, and for establishing a permanent Union between them and Great Britain."[32] At the bottom of the copy, he wrote: "The above Plan I had the honour with Mr. Galloway to lay before my Lord George Germain in March 1780; and had it then been adopted, the Colonies would have now been united with Great Britain." Except for minor changes, this Plan submitted to Dundas in 1788 agreed in all respects with the Galloway-Morrison document of 1780.

In the meantime Galloway was advocating in public the adoption of the Plan of Union of 1774, even though it was contradictory in some essential points to that submitted to Germain. He was careful, however, to point out that the Plan presented to the Continental Congress did not represent his own convictions, but merely what he thought the Congress could be induced to accept. This he did in his examination before the Committee on American Papers in 1779 and again in the reprinting of his *Candid Examination* in 1780. His failure to receive encouragement from the aging Germain did not deter him making other attempts upon the ministry. The new Secretary at War, Charles Jenkinson, was another exponent of dealing firmly with America, and he was said to have an immense influence with the King, even greater than that of Lord North. Galloway therefore turned to him.

Charles Jenkinson, member of an old Oxfordshire family, had come into prominence by attracting the attention of Lord Bute with a clever election song in 1760.[33] He became

[32] See below, Appendix 5.
[33] J. A. Hamilton's sketch of Jenkinson in the *Dictionary of National Biography*, XXIX; Doran, *Walpole's Last Journals*, II. 322, 516, 606; *Memoirs of the Public Life . . . of the Right Honourable the* [Second] *Earl of Liverpool* (London, 1827), 6-7; Jenkinson (1727-1808) was made Baron Hawkesbury of Hawkesbury in 1786, and in 1796 was created the Earl of Liverpool.

Bute's private secretary, entered Parliament, and when Bute resigned became leader of the King's Friends in the House of Commons. His intimacy with the royal family was due in part, no doubt, to the fact that he was auditor of accounts to the Princess Dowager of Wales until her death in 1772. He became Secretary at War in 1778, and during the remainder of the North ministry he was reputed to have a very great and secret influence at court, so much so that he was thought to have controlled Lord North's relations with the throne. This brought him a considerable amount of odium, but, since his office did not compare in responsibility with that of Germain, it also helped to magnify his importance. Galloway and other contemporaries may have believed that Jenkinson had a greater influence with the King than did North, but it is now apparent that the belief was ill founded. Jenkinson was befriended by the King, but George III gave to few if any other subjects the affectionate, patient, and devoted friendship that he bestowed upon his first minister. But this undeserved reputation of the Secretary at War, together with his unwearied efforts to prosecute the war with the colonies, must have induced Galloway to approach him with his Plans of Union.

This he did in the form of a letter containing some indication in its careful footnotes and in a reference to a nonexistent appendix that was intended for publication.[34] The letter, though undated, was probably written during the latter part of 1780 or the early part of 1781. Its opening paragraph also indicates that Jenkinson had requested Galloway to submit his ideas on the subject, though, if the manuscript were intended for publication, this may have been merely a literary device to give the appearance of official interest in the matter. What it does indicate, more specifically, is that Galloway had met Jenkinson and had secured his permission to draft such a manuscript. Actually, of course, Galloway already had at hand his two previous Plans of Union—one

[34] See below, Appendix 3.

submitted to the Continental Congress and the other to Lord George Germain. Consequently, since events in America had not changed drastically since he had written to Germain in the spring of 1779, there was presumably little for him to do except redraft the Germain letter, polish his style here and there, and strengthen his arguments.

Actually, however, the Plan of Union submitted to Jenkinson was in many respects a more statesmanlike document than its predecessors. It was written after Galloway had published his *Cool Thoughts, Plain Truth,* and *Historical and Political Reflections*—a fact indicated by his frequent borrowings from those pamphlets and by his footnote citations to them[35]—and his arguments had therefore been sharpened by his conflicts with the Howe brothers and with the Dean of Gloucester. He was, for example, much more positive in urging his first alternative, colonial representation in Parliament, as the most perfect form of union. In his *Historical and Political Reflections* he had said that it was "much to be regretted, that neither country seems to approve of an American representation in Parliament." Now, in his letter to Jenkinson, he argued that the sentiments of people on both sides of the Atlantic were varied and that the practicability of the suggestion could not be determined until it was at least given a trial. He was scarcely correct when he affirmed that the proposal had never been made nor discussed in either country. Nor was he entirely accurate in saying that

A few republicans in America, a very small part of the People, have condemned it, without discussion and without ever consult-

[35] *Letters to a Nobleman on the Conduct of the War in the Middle Colonies* (London, 1779), 6-8, 22, 23, 24; *Cool Thoughts on the Consequences to Great Britain of American Independence* (London, 1780), 13-14, 18, 25, 33-34, 36, 46-47; *Historical and Political Reflections on the Rise and Progress of the American Rebellion in which the Causes of the Rebellion are pointed out and the Policy and Necessity of Offering to the Americans a System of Government founded in the Principles of the British Constitution are Clearly demonstrated* (London, 1780), 24-28, 47, 117, 122, 123-24, 125, 127, 129-30 (this pamphlet contains, at p. 70-81, a summary of the Plan of 1774); *Plain Truth: or, a Letter to the Author of Dispassionate Thoughts on the American War* (London, 1780), 4, 5, 15, 29, 33, 40, 54, 58, 60, 63.

ing the People at large. They would not permit it, with many other Matters of great Importance, to be discussed. And no one to this day can say whether this Country will admit of it, however necessary it may be to the safety and duration of the Empire.

Because of the importance of the subject, Galloway felt that an attempt at representation in Parliament ought to be tried, even though its success would be a matter of uncertainty, for "a failure cannot be mischievous." He evidently felt somewhat more optimistic on this point than when he had written Germain, for he went so far as to tell Jenkinson that if this alternative Plan were adopted, all other parts of his second Plan could be annexed to it save those sections dealing with an American legislature.

The two Plans of Union sent to Jenkinson also differed from those of 1779 in the addition of an article providing that each of the two houses of the American legislature could, with the approval of the Crown representative, elect two commissioners to sit in the corresponding houses of Parliament. These commissioners would have the same privileges as British members of Parliament, except that they would not be entitled to vote. In the Jenkinson Plans, too, Galloway was more emphatic in his argument for transferring the principle of aristocracy, as the British understood and applied that principle, to the American branch of Parliament. "This only," he maintained, "can suppress democratical Intemperance, and reduce popular Influence within its just and constitutional bounds. Nothing else, except Arbitrary and despotic Authority, which cannot be exercised in a mixt form of Government, can possibly answer the purpose." Many, he said, had lately objected to the idea of an American legislature. But would it not be better to establish a legal and constitutional congress, controlled and checked by the principles of monarchy and aristocracy, than "an unconstitutional democratical and independent Congress"? If the colonists had a constitutional body, in which they were represented and to the establishment of which they had agreed, they

[103]

would respect it and not rebel. Benjamin Franklin, in 1789, said much the same about his Albany Plan of 1754.[36]

But Galloway's matured thinking, his concern for justice to the land of his birth, and his statesmanlike views appeared to best advantage in the provisions for commercial regulations in the Plans of Union sent to Jenkinson. There were, he pointed out to Jenkinson, two great questions involved in reconstructing the empire: first, "What is the best system of polity by which America may, in future, be governed by the British State, to the longest period of time?" and second, "What advantages of commerce the Colonists ought to enjoy as Members of that State." The first he considered the more important, as it provided the foundation for the second. In his *Cool Thoughts* Galloway had followed the line of mercantilist thought and argued for "that commerce which a society can command within itself, independent of others," and affirmed the opinion that "No human ties are so binding as those founded in interest."[37] He likewise repudiated as specious the argument of the Dean of Gloucester that a similarity of laws, religion, and manners would insure a continuation of Anglo-American commerce in the old channels even if America achieved independence. But he had maintained in his *Historical and Political Reflections* that "it is not a confederation of force, or a commercial alliance, but a firm and solid union in polity, which only can secure the colonies."[38] Now, in his letter to Jenkinson, he reaffirmed this conviction:

. . . any connection with America merely founded in a commercial treaty can answer no good end to Great Britain. It cannot be stable and permanent. It will change with the circumstances of

[36] Franklin thought that "the . . . separation of the Colonies from the Mother Country might not so soon have happened, nor the Mischiefs suffered on both sides have occurred perhaps during another century . . . [and] the different parts of the Empire might still have remained in Peace and Union" if the Albany Plan had been adopted. *American Museum*, 1789, p. 368; *Penn. Mag. Hist. and Biog.*, XXIII, 269-70.

[37] *Cool Thoughts*, 6, 14-15, 18.

[38] *Hist. and Pol. Reflections*, p. 122.

America which being a new Country is changing every Year, and like a Young Genius, no one can yet form a judgment what it is, or what will be her interest, in respect to Commerce, in half a century. We must not therefore rely on a Commercial Connection without a just system of polity to retain it. For be assured it cannot otherwise be secured by all the inventions of human Wisdom.

Convinced, therefore, of the unfolding future of the young genius of America, Galloway, perhaps in desperation at the thought that the richest part of the empire was about to be lost forever, departed as far as he dared from the Mercantilist philosophy of the Old Empire. If, in refuting the Dean of Gloucester, he had read Adam Smith, he was now willing to concede perhaps more than most Mercantilists would have. At any rate, in that part of his previous Plans of Union granting to the American legislature power to make laws of general concern to the colonies or more than one colony, both in civil and criminal matters, he amended the article to read: "as well civil and Criminal as Commercial." More specifically, he added to each of the two Plans of Union six articles concerning trade and commerce. Far from looking upon the colonies solely as sources of wealth for the parent state, Galloway argued that if the colonies would in the future maintain their peace establishments, support the officers of the Crown according to their rank and dignity, and grant a just proportion of aids towards the national defense, "Great Britain can have in Justice no further pecuniary demands on them as Members of her Society." Obedience to the state would therefore entitle the colonies to equal privileges with the subjects in Great Britain, Scotland, and Ireland, and any unnecessary or unjust distinctions would only bring about jealousies, discord, and ultimately dissolution of the union. In telling language he concluded that "it can be of no Consequence to the State whether a Subject grows rich by Commerce on the Ohio or in Cheapside while it can certainly command a just

[105]

and reasonable proportion of his Wealth whenever necessary to the safety of the Society."

His six commercial articles provided that the trade of the colonies would be subject to the same regulations and restrictions as the trade of Great Britain; that the trade of the colonies with foreign nations would be subject to the same regulations and restrictions, and liable to the same duties on foreign imports, as the trade of Great Britain; that the colonies should have the same privileges of exporting their products as the subjects of Great Britain, except such articles as were necessary to carry on the manufactures of Great Britain and to furnish its navy with naval stores, and these articles should be exported only to England; that the colonies should not interfere in their manufactures with the manufactures of Great Britain, nor should their manufactures be exported to foreign countries; that, upon these principles, Parliament should have sole authority to superintend the navigation of America; and that all previous Acts of Parliament inconsistent with these principles of the Union should be repealed. This, of course, did not represent a radical departure from the modified system of Mercantilism that had existed under the Trade and Navigation Acts of the Old Empire. But it did show that Galloway was willing to attach a moderately liberal provision to his Plan of Union to make it more acceptable to Americans and also, perhaps, to offset the arguments of the Dean of Gloucester.

Tory ministers such as Germain and Jenkinson were none too enthusiastic in their acceptance of the ideas and proposals of American Loyalists, as Galloway had bluntly pointed out in his letter to one of the King's Ministers. Even though the Plan of Union sent to Jenkinson was more carefully prepared and more skilfully argued, it apparently met with the same indifference that Germain had exhibited in 1779. When the news of the British disaster at Yorktown came and was followed by the Peace Treaty of 1783, Galloway and other Loyalists were filled with despair at the thought of their possessions and their native land being lost. But Galloway, who had given so much time and thought to the matter of imperial union, could not give up hope that some workable plan could be devised to bring the Americans back within the circle of British power. Sometime after the Treaty of Peace and after he had been granted a pension by the Loyalist Commission, he set himself once more to the task. Discouragement and resignation were implicit in every line of his opening paragraph:

Few Men, I fear, propose anything in favour of government with a view entirely abstracted from private Interest. And certainly, when such a suspicion prevails, it must throw a disagreeable shade over the offered plan. To prevent therefore all imputations of that kind, I, on honour, do solemnly declare, that I have not a desire for any employment under government. Because, for several reasons, I am persuaded, that it is not in my power, to fill any office with a degree of ardour and reputation at all proportionate to my wishes. My only request now is that His Majesty may suffer an old and faithfull officer, tho nearly ruined by his uniform and constant attachment to his Majesty's government, to retire on what, considering his former style of life & service, can not be deemed extravagant.[39]

The "old and faithfull officer" was in his middle fifties, but he apparently believed that in order to catch the attention of the ministry it was necessary to declare oneself to be a disinterested advocate.

The exact date of this Plan of Union is not known, though it was probably about 1785. Nor is it known to whom it was addressed, nor whether, in fact, it was ever brought to the notice of an officer of government. Shelburne, as noted above, had received documents from Galloway in 1782 and had transmitted them to the King. George III had advised Shelburne to show some civility to Galloway, and this indication of royal interest may have led Galloway to make one further attempt upon the Whig ministry. The manuscript of this Plan

[39] See Appendix 4.

of Union is a very rough draft, showing many corrections, interlineations, and changes. In style and in content it differs considerably from the preceding Plans. One paragraph in it is revealing: Galloway felt that it was beyond his abilities to give a complete draft of the necessary and desirable plan; that none should attempt such an important task except "such as have their heads and hearts more entire and more at ease than I can boast of"; and that his "want of every book necessary to assist my memory, and inform my judgment, will abridge my observations." In many ways, therefore, this Plan of Union is more interesting because of its obviously disinterested approach, and especially because of its being written under circumstances separating Galloway somewhat from his favorite writers on government and even from his own controversial pamphlets. Stripped of these supports, the Plan may be regarded as reflecting Galloway's own convictions more precisely than his previous writings on the subject.

If so, it reveals a mind grown more conservative with adversity and age. It is not altogether clear whether Galloway intended his "general hints" toward "a permanent and happy constitution in his Majesty's colonies on the Continent of America" to apply to the revolted provinces or whether he had in mind only those that remained in the empire. He may have hoped for the former, but there was no suggestion of reducing the colonies by military force and there is, in one passage of his remarks, evidence that he had accepted the verdict of Yorktown. But to whatever portion of the British empire in America his Plan applied, it reflected the conservative desire for stricter imperial control in almost every relation with the colonies. This was true not merely in the structure of government proposed for the colonies, but also in the provisions for controlling and more effectively suppressing any incipient disloyalty to the crown. In the place of an American branch of the British Parliament, there was to be a Lord Lieutenant or Governor General and Council, both to be appointed by the Crown and the latter to hold office during good behavior. All of the colonies were to be reduced to one general form of government, and over them the Governor General and Council were to have control. This, in short, was transferring to the colonies the principles of monarchy and aristocracy without the important element corresponding to the House of Commons. The Governor General and Council were to have power to call any or all of the colonial governors before them to furnish information; power to reprimand or suspend such governors; power, in the case of sudden emergencies such as insurrection, to direct and order the governors how to act; power to command and direct the military forces within the colonies, both on land and sea; and, most extraordinary of all, power to control all laws, "both temporal and perpetual," made within the colonies. Whereas the Germain and Jenkinson Plans had permitted the individual colonies to make their own laws concerning internal police, this provided that the Governor General and Council should have a hand in such legislation, though in the case of any laws vetoed by them, appeal could lie to the King. In essence, what Galloway was trying to do here was to transfer to America a full representation of the executive branch of the British government so as to avoid, so far as possible, the delays and dangers arising from the great distance that separated the colonies from the mother country. He was well aware of the fact that the American provinces had frequently enacted laws for temporary advantages, even though they were certain of meeting the royal veto. Often, too, in colonial administration, local circumstances had "shifted so suddenly and violently between the giving information, and receiving instructions how to act, as entirely to change the immediate and proper objects of attention."

Thus, as had happened with so many British conservatives and American Loyalists, the humiliating fact of the American Revolution drove Galloway to the extreme position of trying to avoid the threat of revolution by using more and more of the methods that had produced one. A closer supervision of imperial administration in 1763 had produced a revolution that, to the legalists and the conservatives, was unjustifiable and incomprehensible. But that lesson, so costly to the British Empire, was lost upon her statesman and upon conservatives like Galloway, as Lord Durham so clearly demonstrated half a century later. Consequently, not satisfied with suggesting a form of imperial government that was totally unrepresentative of the people, Galloway proposed to go much further in circumscribing individual liberty and in suppressing the popular will. He proposed that all civil and military officers, all heads of colleges, all students and fellows, and all lawyers should take oaths of allegiance to the state, including a clause promising obedience to all laws of Parliament relating to the British colonies, excepting only laws taxing real or personal property. But the power of Parliament to regulate trade in the colonies, "by levying such duties from, or entirely prohibiting such parts of it, as from time to time, they shall think fit, must be acknowledged and recognized by such officers and others in as strong terms as the English language can furnish." Other reactionary proposals provided for property qualifications for voting or holding office, limiting the number of representatives in assemblies, and limiting or dispersing town meetings when they exceeded their powers. Galloway's old conviction that the Presbyterians were fomenters of republicanism also led him to suggest that "In all colledges and other public seminaries of learning Caution ought to be used to prevent the principal trusts being lodged in the hands of gentlemen whose religious tenets point them decidedly to republicanism."

Galloway could scarcely have put the reactionary point of view of the British imperialist of the 1780's more succinctly. The postulates were simple: political disaffection could be avoided by stricter political control, by limiting suffrage, and by denying participation in government to those who were potentially disaffected; subversive ideas, and the teaching of

[110]

such ideas, could be controlled by the simple expedient of controlling appointments to institutions of learning. Had Galloway's Plans prevailed, he would have been ranked by history among the first of British imperial statesmen. But a determined people, sure of themselves and of their destiny, thrust aside any ideas or any men impeding their road to the future. Failing to understand the meaning and direction of the American people, the Exile gained from them, in return for his misguided patriotism, not understanding but hatred and misfortune. Devoted to historic institutions, the Conservative purchased of history, in return for his devotion, not fame but obscurity.

THE PLAN OF UNION OF 1774[1]

A plan of a proposed Union between Great Britain and the Colonies of New Hampshire, The Massachusets Bay, Rhode Island, Connecticut, New York, New Jersey, Pensylvania, Maryland, the three lower Counties on Delaware, Virginia, North Carolina, South Carolina and Georgia.

THAT a British and American Government[2] for regulating the Administration of the general Affairs of America be proposed and

[1] James Duane Papers, New York Historical Society. Endorsed in the handwriting of James Duane: "Mr Galloway's Motion & Plan of Union, proposed in Congress 28th Septr 1774. Seconded & supported by the New York Delegates. But finally rejected and ordered to be left out of the minutes. Jas. Duane." Burnett, *op. cit.*, I. 51 *n.*, is of the opinion that this draft of the Plan of Union of 1774 is "in an unidentified clerical hand." In my opinion the document is in Galloway's handwriting, being the same as that in part of the Plans of Union in Appendices 2, 3, and 4. It differs from the version given in Ford, ed., *Journals of the Continental Congress,* I. 49, as Burnett has pointed out, chiefly in the heading: the draft in the Duane Papers enumerates by name all of the colonies, whereas the version given in the *Journals* omits this enumeration. There are other minor differences in phraseology.

This draft in the Duane Papers is accompanied by a resolution, also in Galloway's handwriting, providing for submitting the Plan on appeal to the King and Parliament, without first recommending it to the colonies (the second version of this resolution—the so-called William Franklin version—provided that the Plan be submitted to the various colonies for approval; *Journals,* I. 48-49). Galloway said in his examination before the House of Commons that this first version, "in my own handwriting, which identically was delivered by me in Congress . . . is endorsed in the hand of Charles Thomson, the then and present secretary to Congress"; Ford, ed., *Journals,* I. 44. But in the copy of this resolution in the Duane Papers, there is an endorsement by Duane reading as follows: "Resolves intended to be offerd by Mr. Galloway & seconded by J. D. for Promoting a Plan of Union between G. B. & A. But as the Plan itself was rejected by the Congress; the Resolves became fruitless & were not proposed." A copy of the so-called Franklin version is attached to Galloway's own version in the Duane Papers, and this endorsement by Duane presumably refers to the established in America, including all the said Colonies; within and under which Government each Colony shall retain its present Constitution and powers of regulating and governing its own internal Police in all Cases whatsoever.

That the said Government be administer'd by a president General to be appointed by the King and a Grand Council to be chosen by the Representatives of the people of the several Colonies in their respective Assemblies, once in every three years.

That the several Assemblies shall choose Members for the Grand Council in the following Proportions—viz.

> New Hampshire
> Massachusets Bay
> Rhode Island
> Connecticut
> New York
> New Jersey
> Pensylvania
> Delaware Counties
> Maryland
> Virginia
> North Carolina
> South Carolina
> Georgia

Who shall meet at the City of   for the first Time being called by the President General as soon as conveniently may be after his Appointment.

That there shall be a new Election of Members for the Grand Council every three years, and on the Death Removal or Resignation of any Member his place shall be supplied by a new Choice at the next sitting of the Assembly of the Colony he represented. That the Grand Council shall meet once in every year if they shall think it necessary, and oftener if occasion shall require, at such Time and place as they shall adjourn to at the last preceeding Meeting, or as they shall be called to meet at by the president General in any Emergency.

---

former, otherwise his endorsement appears to be contradictory to Galloway's statement before the House of Commons; Burnett, *op. cit.*, I. 51 *n.*

[2] The word *"Legislature"* is written above the word "Government."

That the grand Council shall have power to choose their Speaker and shall hold and exercise all the like Rights Liberties and privileges as are held and exercised by and in the House of Commons of Great Britain.

That the president General shall hold his office during the pleasure of the King, and his Assent shall be requisite to all Acts of the Grand Council and it shall be his Office and duty to cause them to be carried into Execution.

That the president General by and with the Advice and Consent of the Grand Council hold & exercise all the Legislative Rights, Powers and Authorities necessary for regulating and administering all the general Police & Affairs of the Colonies in which Great Britain and the Colonies of any of them, the Colonies in general or more than one Colony are in any Manner concerned as well civil and criminal as commercial.

That the said president General and Grand Council be an inferior and distinct Branch of the British Legislature united and incorporated with it for the aforesaid general purposes; and that any of the said general Regulations may originate and be formed and digested either in the Parliament of Great Britain or in the said Grand Council, and being prepared transmitted to the other for their Approbation or Dissent and that the Assent of both shall be requisite to the validity of all such general Acts or Statutes.

That in Time of War all Bills for granting Aids to the Crown prepared by the Grand Council and approved by the president General shall be valid and passed into a Law without the Assent of the British parliament.[3]

[3] This Plan of Union was printed in Galloway's *Candid Examination* (New York, 1775 and London, 1780); in T. B. Chandler's *What Think Ye of the Congress Now?* (New York, 1775, and London, 1775); and is to be found in *N. J. Archives*, 1st. ser., X. 504-507. Cf. *American Archives*, I, and *Works of John Adams*, II. 387-91.

TWO PLANS OF UNION

Set forth in a Letter from Joseph Galloway to Lord George Germain March 18, 1779[1]

PLANS for Establishing a Permanent UNION between *GREAT BRITAIN* and *AMERICA*

FIRST PLAN

1st A REPRESENTATION in Parliament as in the cases of Chester, Durham, Wales and Scotland.

Remarks

THIS plan is to be prefer'd to all others because it forms the most perfect Union. Unity in Legislation, or the agreement of the people to obey in all things one supreme will or power, is that policy which alone forms the Society, and creates that cement or Bond which can only bind and tye its members together. It is also that principle which the Capacity or power of Collecting and Commanding the whole strength of the several parts of the Community for its preservation and Defence is founded. Without it the State can hold no security in obtaining those aids which are necessary to enable it to preserve the internal peace or external protection, nor has it the power of promoting and establishing a similarity of Laws, Regulations and policy, which is necessary to create the sameness of Customs, Habits and Manners, among the people, which fixes the national attachment and the Harmony and uniformity of sentiments, that induce them to Act as one Body in all Matters where their common welfare is concerned. The Idea of two supreme and independent powers in the same Society is so contrary to the essential principles of Union

[1] Stopford-Sackville MSS, William L. Clements Library. The letter from Galloway to Germain which accompanied these Plans of Union is discussed at length in Chapter V.

upon which all Societys are formed and so inconsistent with the natural law and Design of Government that it is utterly inadmissible and absurd.

A Separation in Legislature gives us the most perfect Idea of two Independent Societys. These are only distinguishable by the Distinct obedience which their Subjects owe to their Several and respective Supreme Heads. The Subjects of each other cannot obey the orders and Regulations of Both, which will rarely be the same, and often contradictory. If they yield obedience to one, they cannot be subjects or members of the other, & a seperation in some things and not in others is what never was yet established, because inconsistent with that unity of Power which constitutes the Essence of Supreme Authority. And to admit of it in the Article of Taxation is to give it up in the most important point, in that upon which the Strength and Defence of the Society entirely depends. It would be more wisdom to allow it in every other article of Regulation, and to reserve that of Taxation. Because should we intend to give a part of the Society the most effectual means of Separating itself from the principal Community, none could be invented so perfectly to answer the purpose as the Right to Levy Taxes and receive Money independent of the State.

This unity in Legislature is most perfect in absolute Monarchy, because its powers are Single, pure and Unmixed, and not liable to Faction or controul in its Deliberations, nor Delaying their Execution, and could mankind be certain of always Placing on the Throne a prince of Wisdom and Goodness reason would certainly instruct them to prefer it, on this account only, to all other Forms. But as they have found this impossible, they have in order to preserve their rights from the violence of wicked and Corrupt Monarchs, constituted Checks on their Power by a mixture of a Share of their own in the Supreme Legislative Council. But in this Compound Kind of Government, they have ever found it necessary to the Strength of the Society and permanent Union of its Members to preserve this Unity in the Supreme Legislature as perfect as possibly, consistent with the nature of the Government. It was upon a knowledge of these principals and their Effects that the Romans acted when they abolished their first form of Government, and established their second, and our Ancestors, in forming the present Constitution of England, The Union between England and Scotland, and in granting representation in parliament to the Malcontents in Wales Chester and Durham. The peace and Harmony and perfect submission of those places ever since are so many evident proofs of the salutary effects of that policy. To this may be added another Example. The Roman Colonies revolted from the principal State because they were bound by the Laws and Orders of the Senate in which they were not represented—as they were not enterd in their comitia or enrolled in their Legions. They petitioned for the Privileges of Roman Citizens in vain. They took to Arms and had almost destroyed the Power of Rome. At length upon these Rights being granted, a perfect Union and Harmony took place which lasted as long as the Empire continued.

A SECOND PLAN OF UNION &c.

If a Representation in Parliament cannot be obtained from objections arising on either side, then it is proposed that an American Branch of the British Legislature be established in America. 1st That this Branch consist of a perfect Representative of the Crown, an upper House and a representation of the People. The first to be appointed by the Crown. The Members of the second to be appointed in like manner, vested with some degree of Rank or Dignity above the Commons, and to hold their offices during Life, unless removed by the concurrent impeachment or address of the King's Representative and the lower House. And the members of the third to be chosen by the assemblies of the Several Colonies.

2nd That this Branch of Legislature be considered as an Inferior branch of the British Legislature, united and incorporated with it for the General purposes herein after mentioned; and that it be established, that any of the said Regulations may originate and be digested either in the parliament of Great Britain or in the American Houses; and being Prepared transmitted to the other for its approbation or Dissent and that the assent of both be requisite to the validity of all such regulations.

3rd That the Jurisdiction of the American Branch be confined to such Regulations as relate to the General police of the Colonies

[117]

in which Great Britain and the Colonies, the Colonies in General, or more than one Colony are concerned, as well civil criminal as commercial.

4th   That the Right of Calling, prorogueing and adjourning this Branch of the Legislature be in the Crown.

Remarks

1st   If unity in Legislation be absolutely necessary to the union and Safety of the Empire, and it cannot be procured by a representation in parliament, there is no other mode of obtaining it ever yet invented but by forming a new Branch and incorporating it with the Parliament, by mixing their Jurisdiction together, & making the *assent of both* necessary to the validity of their acts. It is this *Joint assent* that forms the Unity of parliament and of all other mixed Forms of Government. In some we find two, others three, four and five, Branches, thus incorporated. An increase in number of Branches, is indeed not desirable, if it could be avoided. It renders the System less perfect and the Transaction of Business more dilatory and difficult. But these are difficulties which must give way to greater, and to necessity, and perhaps in the present plan they will be found less than on any other except the one first proposed.

2nd   This union will not be absolutely perfect, because the Jurisdiction of the American House, will not extend to the affairs of Great Britain. These will remain the objects of Parliamentary Decision and regulation, and yet it will affectually answer the two great purposes in view of preserving the Rights of the Colonies and keeping them Dependant Members of the parent State. No Infringement of their Rights can take place without their assent, and by mixing the Jurisdiction of their House with the British, no Regulations Beneficial or necessary to their Interest and welfare can be adopted without the consent of Parliament. The one will secure the Rights, and the other their Connection with and Dependance on Great Britain. Great Britain will possess an independant Legislature of her own and hold an essential Share in that of America which will establish her Subordination.

3rd   But Great Britain will have a further and very important Security for the Dependance of America. The Crown will remain forever seated in Great Britain. Its powers and perogatives must all flow from thence; and yet will be equally extended to and prevail in America. The Military Power— The Strong Posts, Forts and Garrisons, and all appointments, civil and Military, Honorable and lucrative, will remain in its possession and flow from it; by which means a great weight and influence may be established in America centering in Great Britain, so as to prevent any future attempt in the former to throw off her connection and Dependance on the Latter.

4th   It may be objected that the Americans by this Plan will have Sufficient Security for their Rights; But that the crown will have no certainty that the aids will be granted when the wants and Defence of the Empire require them. The answer is that there is more political and Rational Security that the aids will be granted under this Plan than in the Mode of requisitions of the several Assemblies so often proposed, under a Total Exemption from parliamentary Taxation. This mode has been often tried and its absurdity proved by experience, at a time when the Parliamentary Authority was not disputed or intended so to be, but hung over the Colonies in *Terrorem*. And when the Colonies were in the most eminent Danger of being Conquered by a foreign Enemy, altho every encouragement was given to allure them to a discharge of their Equitable and necessary Duty, Some granted the aids required in one year others in another, and some gave none during the war. And indeed this conduct in the Colonies was to be expected, as the causes arose naturally out of that policy upon which their late connection with the principal State is founded. This mode may be tried again but the same causes will ever produce the same effects and the same if not greater Delinquencies will be the Result so that the present plan cannot be worse but upon Examination it may be found to be better.

5th   By this Plan the causes of the Colonies failing in granting the necessary Aids will be removed—one arose from the disunited State of the Colonies and want of any mode by which their Just Quotas could be ascertained, another from the Disputes between the Proprietary Governors and their assemblies respecting the Taxation of the proprietary Estate and other matters; A Third from the Local Situation of the Colony, it being remote from immediate Danger and Invasion by the Enemy, and the fourth arose from the want of some General Authority having Jurisdiction over the whole to ascertain their respective Quotas and compell them to do their reasonable and necessary Duty. Under the present plan, the power of Granting Aids are placed in other Hands, before whom none of those mischevious disputes can happen and Competent besides to the removal of all other Difficulties.

6th   It is in this Plan a Fundamental Stipulation and condition of the Union that whenever Great Britain shall give   towards the National Defence, the Colonies shall give in a certain proportion. It is not to be presumed that the American House will wantonly Break the Stipulation, as it is the Great Base of the Union. Besides their Interest and Safety will teach them not to do it. The Enemies of Great Britain will be their Enemies. A War with her will be a war with them and the Ground and Safety of their Happiness the same and not to be seperated. They can give their Money into no other Hand, but those of the Crown without a Convulsion in their Constitution, which must destroy it and if they refuse they must want its Protection. To which may be added that in such case the parliament will have it in its power to refuse its assent to any Beneficial Bills necessary to the Interest and welfare of the Colonies. Thus all former Disputes being adjusted, and Grounds of future excluded, mutual interest and Safety will beget the Desire of Complying with this Great and Fundamental Covenant and of preserving that union and Harmony which is so necessary to the Welfare and Happiness of Both Countries.

7th   The same objection might be made to the Constitution of Parliament. It might be asked with equal Reason what Security has the Crown that the Commons will Grant the necessary aids? The only answer is that it is their Interest so to do, And if they refuse, they Desert their own Safety and must want that protection which was the Great End of their entering into Society. This is all the Security the crown can have in a mixed form of Government; and this it will possess under the plan now proposed.

8th   In order to preserve the same Ballance of Power, between the Crown and the people in America, as in Great Britain, and to give the crown that weight and Influence which it has long wanted in America, it is necessary that the American Branch of the Legislature be established on the principles of a Mix'd Government. An entire Democracy without the checks of Aristocracy and Monarchy would be dangerous to the State. An Aristocracy only would not form an Union, but be too arbitrary. It will therefore be certainly best to Blend the powers and Rights of them all in the American Branch in the same manner as they are Blended in the principal State. Besides it is of the utmost Importance to the permanent Union of the parts of a Great Empire that the same essential principles of policy should pervade the whole should run thro every inferior and Subordinate Politic Body.

There should be no deviation from those upon which the principal State is Settled, be its Form what it may. If it be Monarchial the principles of a Monarchy, if Aristocratical, the principles of Aristocracy, if Democratical the principles of Democracy Should be strictly adhered to in the Forms of all their inferior politic Bodies, and if it be a mixed form of Government, then the principles of all of them should be so Temper'd and mixed together as to admit of no variation from that Policy upon which the principal State is Established. These principles being opponent in their Several Natures to each other they are mixed together to check each others excess and to form a Just Ballance. Every deviation must therefore Destroy the Ballance and weaken the System. The principles of the different forms of Government are so opposite in their natures that they can no more agree than Fire and water. They may indeed be so mixt together by Wisdom and art as to Moderate the violent effects and form a Ballance to each other as a Moist atmosphere will cool a too heated Air and render it fit for respiration. But when they are so injudiciously mixt as to give a Superiority to one over the other, Weakness and Ruin must follow. It is this heterogeneous mixture of contrary Principles not wisely Tempered together which Form a part of the weakness of the British Government. Proof of this Truth might be adduced; but the proprietary and Charter Governments in America afford much Stronger.

5th In Time of War to prevent Delay in the granting extraordinary aids to the Crown Bills for that purpose may be finally passed into Laws by the Kings Representative, being authorized by a temporary Act of Parliament.

6th   The Jurisdiction of the American Branch being Confined to the General Affairs of America, it will be necessary, and, perhaps, good policy to give the Colonial Legislatures the power of regulating their own respective internal Affairs—subject as usual to the Negative of the King in Council.

Remarks

The Multiplicity and Variety of Regulations necessary to the order and welfare of the Colonies would render the Business of Parliament as well as of the American Branch infinite. And it will be perhaps sound policy to confine the American Jurisdiction to General objects only without suffering it to intermeddle with the internal police of the several Colonies.

7th   The peace establishment of each country may be maintained by itself. In America perhaps best by the respective Colonies. But the Aids to be Granted to the Crown by the American Branch should be in proportion as the wealth of one country bears to the other. This proportion may be adjusted by a Comparitive view of the exports of Both.

8th   The proportion of each country being settled it should be a fundamental Stipulation in the Compact of Union, that whenever Great Britain shall give   America shall give   and so in proportion to any greater or lesser sum given by Great Britain. And as the wealth of one country may increase more than the other, it may be further stipulated that when the Exports of America shall rise or fall 20PC her proportion of Aids shall rise or fall in the same proportion.

9th   The appointment of all Governors, Judicial, Ministerial and executive officers, and offices as well those which concern the administration of Justice as the collection receiv'g and paying out the publick Revenues, and of all military officers should be fixed in the Crown. In short the perogatives of the Crown should by no means be lessened or abridged by Union but remain the same in America as in Great Britain.

10th   All acts of assembly which affect the perogatives of the Crown should be repealed or annulled.

[122]

Remarks

There are many acts of the Colonial Assemblies which take away the perogatives of the Crown and place them either in the Hands of the Assemblies or the people at large; such as the Right of Summoning, Dissolving, proroguging and adjourning them, and of appointing Treasurers, Sheriffs, Coroners, Collectors of the public Revenue, Etc, Etc. This weakens the Authority and influence of the Crown and strengthens the power of the people so as to destroy that Ballance of Power which is the Security of a mixt form of Government.

11th   All the Governments of the Several Colonies should be reduced to one Form, and consist of a Governor and privy Council to be appointed by the Crown, and to hold their offices during its pleasure. An upper house of the same appointment and removable on the address of the Governor and Assembiy; and an Assembly chosen by the people.

Remarks

The Provincial Governments especially the proprietary and Charter require great amendments and alterations. The latter are not admissable on any grounds of reason or policy. Their Democratical principles never can accord with those of mixt Monarchy. They destroy the Ballance of its power and never fail to produce factions and Seditions against the Principal State. Men Educated under a popular form of Government and long indulged with excess of liberty never can bear the necessary Rigour of Monarchy, or even of a mixt form of Government. They acquire prejudice in favor of the one they have lived under, believe it is the best Form and that their Happiness can only be secured by it. And this creates an aversion to all others. Here habit becomes second nature and cannot be eradicated, but by contrary customs and practice, & an abolition of the policy under which their former habits were obtained.

It has been observed before that it is of the utmost importance to the duration and strength of a Great Empire that the same principles of Government and policy should pervade all its inferior and Subordinate Members. It is this identity of policy that gives the same spirit to the Laws and creates the same mode of thinking and acting in the People, The Same Customs, Manners, prejudices, attachments and habits so as to form, as it were, one people of one mind in respect of their own Safety and Happiness. It is the True Source from whence spring all national attachments, and these prejudices, we find, in men living under the worst and most slavish Forms of Government. What is that induces a Frenchman, a Turk The Slave of a bashaw whose life is at the disposal of his master to prefer an Existence under their Tyrants to all other Forms of Government? It cannot be the freedom they possess. It is the effect of certain policy, and habits produced by it. They have been Educated under and accustomed to oppression. That which would be intolerable to one not enured to it, becomes by habit easy to them and not only tolerable but preferable to that Liberty which is founded on different policy Manners and customs which they know not how to assume. If those Sentiments be just and Government does not wish to efface all national attachments and to nourish, in its stead, an aversion to the present form of Government and the seeds of faction and Disunion in the Bowels of the Empire, all Democratical and Charter Governments must be abolished.

For the same Reasons the proprietary Governments ought to be changed into Royal. Long experience has proved that the Exercise of the prerogatives of the Crown ought not to be Trusted in the Hands of independent Subjects. They ought not to be, nor are they by Law Grantable in Fee, they are not Transferable at all. The Heir inheriting them may be either a weak or a Bad man. They are not in safe keeping in the hands of the first, and are dangerous weapons in those of the last. Like a Dark cloud between the King and his people, They exclude the Rays of Royalty and prevent that respect and attachment which ensures that obedience that every subject ought to possess for his Sovereign. Their power being independent of the Crown, they consider it as their own; And they make use of it to serve the purposes of their own ambition and Interest and forget that they hold it in Trust for the Honor of the Crown and Good of its People. If they surrender it up to gratify the people they receive the Rewards of Gratitude and affection for it and some times of Interest. If they make use of it to oppress and injure the Subject the Blame and

Odium falls upon the Crown. There are many instances where the most important prerogatives of the Crown have been sacrifised to proprietary Interest and the Humour of the people. Nor would it be difficult to prove that the weight of proprietary Power and influence has been used against the Crown in the present Contest between Great Britain and the Colonies. And it will be found upon a candid inquiry that the prevalence of the Aristocratical as well as Democratical principles of the proprietary and Charter Governments in America has formed the Great Source from whence the present Rebellion has Sprung. Had these Governments been originally formed upon the same principles of mix't policy upon which the principal State is established America had not known a Rebellion.

General Remarks

Should the military Force of the Congress be once reduced their civil Authority and that of every inferiour State will fall of course; and the old Forms of Government being destroyed by the People's own Act as well as forfeited by the Rebellion the whole Country will be in a State of Nature without a Civil Constitution—a perfect Blank until a new Policy shall be established. And upon a View of the present Parties in America it will be found perhaps more easy to constitute new Systems of Government than to restore the old. These Circumstances present the most favorable Opportunity of establishing such a general System of Civil Authority as well as of inferior and subordinate Governments as shall be best calculated to preserve and perpetuate the Union between the two Countries.

America is now divided into two Parties, one of whom nothing less will satisfy them than perfect Independence because they are actuated by Views of Ambition & private Interest. The other who ardently wish for a perpetual Union between G. Britain and the Colonies upon principles of Liberty & Sound Policy, from a conviction that their own Safety & Happiness depend upon it. The one is a meer republican Party firmly attached to democratical Government, and have therefore vested the Powers of all their new States originally and ultimately in the People. The other as firmly adhere to a mixt form of Government, which

[125]

equally guard against the Abuse of Power in the Sovereign and the Licentiousness of the People. And altho the party first mentioned by a Variety of adventitious and favorable Circumstances has been enabled to assume the Power over the other; Yet as the last contains a very great majority of the men of property and of the Colonists in general, who being secluded from all Share in Government, and having suffered in the extreme under a Power in which they have no participation, would willingly embrace any Proposals which afford a rational prospect of relieving them from their distress and ensuring future liberty and safety.

Upon this Brief State of American Parties it will certainly be the best Policy to propose and adopt that System of civil Government which is most agreeable to the people and Promises the most lasting Union between the two Countries—Whether the Prejudices of the Colonists against a Representation in Parliament may not be so fixt as not to be removed upon a full and fair discussion is uncertain. But should this be the case they have imbibed no Prejudices against an American Legislature incorporated with the Parliament. Many men of the best understanding weight and influence in the Colonies wish it had been adopted by the Congress when proposed, And even a majority of that Body before they had fixt their Resolution to be independent, publicly approved and supported it.

The grand Foundation of the Union being settled the other Articles of lesser Consequence to America will be easily adjusted, especially if the Resolution of Government be to extend the same measure of power & freedom to the Colonies as in G. Britain. These will be principles fixt and unalterable to refer to in case of objection & dispute. The prerogatives of the Crown, the Rights of the Subject, and the Ballance which holds the security of both, are well defined and ascertained in the Constitution of the English Government. These may and ought to be made the Tests of Decision. To this the Americans can have no just objection nor hold any argument against it, because an extension of these principles to America is the only means of giving to them the same liberties that are enjoyed by their fellow subjects in G. Britain and of establishing a permanent security for their freedom and a lasting Union between the two Countries.

TWO PLANS OF UNION

Set forth in a Letter from Joseph Galloway
to Charles Jenkinson ca. *1780*[1]

SIR,

In conformity to your request, I have, in the following Sheets, committed my Sentiments to Writing, on the subject of an Union between Great Britain and America. I fear I have greatly exceeded the limits to which you was pleased to confine me. If I have, it has been with the sole design of giving you just information, of the true circumstances of America and the real wishes of its people. And I have done this with the greater satisfaction; because I trust that their desires rightly and fully understood will strictly accord with the real interest and future safety of the Empire. Acting upon these principles, I can rely, with confidence, on your goodness to find, in the rectitude of my intentions, an apology for the length of this address.

The two great Questions involved in this subject are, 1ˢᵗ What is the best system of polity by which America may, in future, be governed by the British State, to the longest period of time? And, secondly, what advantages of commerce the Colonists ought to injoy as Members of that State?—The first Question is of the

[1] Original in the possession of Lawrence J. Morris, Esq., of Philadelphia. As to the provenance of the manuscript, nothing is known save that it was purchased a few years ago from Messrs. Henry Stevens, Son & Stiles, who gave it as their opinion that the corrections in the text, the final paragraph, the signature, and the name of the recipient are all in the handwriting of Galloway. With this opinion I am in agreement. The manner in which Galloway appended footnotes indicates that he may have intended it for publication. Whether this was true or not, whether Jenkinson received it, whether he gave any opinion of it in writing to the author, and whether I am correct in ascribing it to the latter part of 1780 or sometime in 1781 may possibly be ascertained when access can be secured to the collection of Liverpool Manuscripts in the British Museum.

greatest importance, because it not only lays the foundation upon which the second ought to be established, but involves those principles of Civil polity by which the Members of a State can only be combined and solidly bound together in a durable Union.

Before I proceed in the first, you will give me leave to observe in general, that any connection with America merely founded in a commercial treaty can answer no good end to Great Britain. It cannot be stable and permanent. It will change with the circumstances of America which being a new Country is changing every Year, and like a Young Genius, no one can yet form a judgment what it is, or what will be her interest, in respect to Commerce, in half a Century. We must not therefore rely on a Commercial Connection without a just system of polity to retain it. For be assured it cannot otherwise be secured by all the inventions of human Wisdom.

And permit me further in general to observe, that while France, Spain, Portugal, and the other powers in Europe, shall retain their foreign Dominions, and shall hold them secured not only against foreign Invasion, by their Arms but firmly bound by all the political ties of just subordination, arising from the establishment of Principles peculiar to their respective forms of Government, the bad and ruinous policy to Great Britain of giving to her Colonies independence, or any other terms which shall loosen the bands of their subordination to the principal state, and enable them in a little time to become independent, must be too obvious to call for discussion.[2]

But did not this reason subsist in full force, there is another of great weight. The great bulk of the People of America, whose dispositions ought and must, upon every principle of reason and sound policy, be consulted, dread a separation in polity from this Country, and are distressed at the prospect of independence. Their wishes accord with what either is or ought to be those of the people of this Country. They desire to be bound on principles of liberty and policy, yet more firmly than ever, to the principal State, by an enjoyment of the same Rights and Privi-

[2] Cf. *Cool Thoughts*, 13-14, 33-34; *Plain Truth*, 4-5, 11-14.

[128]

ledges, and by being governed by the same measure of power, modified in the same manner as their fellow Subjects enjoy, and are governed by in Great Britain.

If such are the desires of the great bulk of the People of America, it is certainly the interest of Great Britain to gratify them. Because it is by that gratification alone Great Britain can retain and make them useful Members of her Society. It is a reasonable gratification because they ask no more than what subsists in every Civilized Society in the World save in the British Empire. And that which they ask is the only thing necessary to restore the Order and Vigor of the British State Viz^t. to cement and tie the Members of the Empire together and at all times to lead them to act in concert for the common good and safety.

If any knowledge and instruction is to be learnt from the experience of mankind, from the dictates of reason, or from the established maxims and documents of all learned authors who have wrote on Government, this truth will be found, on strict examination, most evident, that the present distraction and convulsions in the British Empire have arisen solely from a system of polity which has been inadvertently adopted in America within the two last Centuries. A system in which the principal State or rather its representatives and trustees have given away, without authority, those powers which were vested in it for the purposes of its own Sovereignty; have relinquished them to the very Persons over whom they ought to be exercised; have instituted inferior Societies totally inconsistent with the Principles upon which the principal State is founded, with powers never intended, and which never can be safely trusted in the hands of the governed. By this means their Attachment to the Principal State has been aliened, and their connection with it dissolved. The powers and the Energy of Government are enfeebled and rendered inadequate to the purposes for which they were originally instituted, and the component parts of the most beautiful, if not the most powerful system in the World are separated from their respective orders and so jumbled together as to produce infinite confusion, and to threaten it with utter dissolution.

It is not difficult for a Person who will look into the nature of Government, to perceive that this dissolution will, in no great

[129]

length of time, take place unless the principal State shall regain
the powers which it ought to possess, which is necessary to its
Authority, and which have been thus illegally, inadvertently and
improperly, granted away. As to the policy of doing it no Man
can doubt it, and as to the right, it is too obvious to admit of
opposition from any but Men of cavalling dispositions. No Man
of sense will assert, that the Kings of this Realm had a right to
grant to the governed the very powers which were intended and
appointed to govern them—to grant away the legislative Authority of the State—to grant Charters with powers destructive of the
mixt form of Government and of that balance which forms the
great foundation of its liberty and safety, and which equally constitutes the great Mounds and barriers against the encroachments
of Tyranny and Licentiousness. There was no such Authority
ever delegated to them. On the contrary it was a breach of their
Trust and void in reason and in Law.

However it is fortunate that from every thing we see at present
this discussion seems unnecessary. The prospect before us pre-
sents us with well grounded hopes that these powers, so injudiciously parted with, may be regained without murmur and with
the assent of nine tenths of the people to whom they have been
granted. A predisposition in them for many years past to the
measure—the additional experience they have had of the Mischiefs under their democratical forms of Government, the dis-
tresses of War which have lessened the pride and sunk the high
demands of the republican Party to the par of reason and sound
policy, all will conspire to render this period the favorable and
happy opportunity.

To satisfy ourselves of the truth of this disposition in the Colonies to be more solidly united with this Country upon constitutional principles we must look into the Conduct of y° People at
large, where we shall find the most evident demonstrations of it.
The Congress were appointed by a small part of the People
["(See Mr Galloway's examination)" deleted.—Ed.] on whose
minds mistaken Ideas of British injustice had made the greatest
Impression. The other, the greater and more sensible part, totally disapproving of every kind of illegal opposition to Government. And yet we find from their instructions to their dele-

[130]

gates founded in these Impressions that they breath nothing but the strongest recommendations of a lasting connection with Great Britain upon constitutional principles.[3] M[r] Galloways examination vid. Note P. 2, and Letters to a Nobleman in the Appendix.

The Congress themselves, tho' composed of a Majority of Men who had the Independence of the Colonies in View, did not dare to depart from this ground contrary to the general sense of the People until they had disarmed them and established their own Power. They therefore claim in behalf of the People all the "Rights, Liberties, Priviledges and Immunities of the free and natural born subjects within the Realm of England." They assert their right to the "extension and benefit of the Common Law," and of "such of the English Statutes as existed at the time of their Colonization and were found applicable to their several local and other circumstances."—And in a variety of their proceedings, they further declare, that their opposition to Government, "had no other objects than the security of the Civil Rights of the Constituent parts of the Empire and the preservation of a happy and lasting connection with Great Britain on salutary and constitutional principles."[*]

In further conformity to this disposition the People at large, and the Men of property, almost universally, to show their detestation of the new forms of Government and their desire of a more firm Union with Great Britain, have altogether seceded from voting in the Election of their Officers, and from accepting of any office of honor profit or trust under them. Rather than unite in the rebellious opposition to Government, they are, with a patience unparallelled, submitting to every species of want, Tyranny and Distress. And as they have not the power, being naked and disarmed, to rid themselves of their oppression, they are constantly looking up to the force of Great Britain for relief, and for that protection against the like mischiefs in future, which

[3] Cf. *Letters to a Nobleman,* 7-11, 22, 23-24; *Examination . . . by . . . the House of Commons,* 6-7, *passim; Historical and Political Reflections,* 129-30. In his examination by the committee of the House of Commons Galloway accused the leaders in Congress of being disingenuous in asserting, in their resolutions and instructions, that they abhorred independence, whereas, according to Galloway, from the time of the French and Indian war on they had been secretly planning and working toward that end.

[*] See their Letter to the Inhabitants of Quebeck.

they are sensible can flow from nothing but a more firm solid and just subordination of the Colonies upon constitutional principles, to the principal State.

And it is an incontestible truth, that the Terms offered by the last Commission, so far as they were explained and understood, were universally disapproved by the Americans.[4] I do not believe they met with the Approbation of one Man in all the Colonies who was capable of looking into their Consequences. The great bulk of the People, the Men of sense and property, who were attached to Great Britain, reprobated them, because they relinquished the established authority of the State over the Colonies: Because they lost sight of those principles upon which its policy was founded: Because they gave up the Rights of the Crown and established no rational system of Polity and Government between the two Countries but on the contrary laid a sure foundation for the future independence of America—And the small Republican party rejected them, because they did not amount to immediate and perfect independence; which they at that time hoped they should obtain through the aid of France.

Under these circumstances we must not take the wishes of the people of America from the Congress. They are not the Representatives of America, but Usurpers whose interest it is, and whose resolution it has been from the beginning, to conceal and misrepresent them, and in defiance of Great Britain and the Peo-

[4] The Carlisle Commission of 1778. See Burnett, *op. cit.*, III, *passim* and "The Manuscripts of the Earl of Carlisle, preserved at Castle Howard," *Hist. MSS. Com., Fifteenth Report, Appendix, Part VI* (London, 1897), 322-420, *passim*. A pamphlet entitled *A Letter to the People of America, lately printed at New York; now Re-published by an American. With a Postscript, by the Editor, Addressed to Sir W . . . . H . . . .* (London, 1778) has been attributed to Galloway by Sabin. This pamphlet was doubtless a part of the propaganda inspired if not produced by the Carlisle Commission, but since it was written after Oct. 3, 1778, and since its style and its ideas do not altogether agree with Galloway's, I am inclined to question the attribution: *e.g.*, the three suggestions for settling the issue by constitutional means were: (1) by taxation powers reserved constitutionally to the individual colonies; (2) by vice-roy from England with an upper house and a lower house joined in an American legislature ("There are so few objections to this form of government, that if it had been proposed by America, the project would have met with no opposition." p. 47-48); (3) representation of America in Parliament. The postscript to Howe is more in accord with Galloway's style and opinion.

ple themselves to maintain their usurpation. They were lately
Men of the least Consequence in their respective Societies. They
have rose by a variety of falsehoods and frauds from Poverty to
Wealth and from the lowest Insignificance into Power; and should
they lose their present Authority they must sink into yet lower
Insignificance and Contempt. They have every thing to lose, but
nothing to gain, by a treaty. It is therefore contrary to reason to
expect that they will treat at all, until they shall utterly despair
of supporting their Power, and the forlorn Hope shall stare them
in the face. And when this shall happen the People themselves,
over whom their Tyranny has been usurped, and who are to be
hereafter bound, are most certainly the Persons pointed out by
reason and good policy to be treated with. Had Charles the second taken his Ideas of the State and wishes of the British Nation
from Cromwell and his Faction and entred into a Treaty with
them he never would have recovered his Kingdom nor restored
the British Constitution.

Plans for establishing a permanent Union between Great
Britain and America.

FIRST PLAN

1st A Representation of the American Colonies in parliament as in the Cases of Chester Durham Wales and
Scotland.

Remarks

This Plan is certainly to be preferred to all others because it forms the most perfect union.

Government is a politic Body consisting of a Head and a variety
of Members of greater and less Utility, Dignity and Importance.
The Union of its parts is formed by, and consists in, the Obedience which all of them are bound to pay to one supreme will and
direction. This is the first great and essential principle upon
which all Societies are formed, and without which none ever did
or can exist. The legislative Authority of every State is the Head
or Supreme will and the inferior Corporations and Politic Bodies,
the officers of Government and the Confederated individuals are

its Members.[5] One supreme Will or Legislative Authority is therefore as necessary and essential to the regular movements, Oeconomy and Energy, of the Politic Body as one Head or rational Will is to the human Body. It is this Unity in the supreme Power and the Obligations of Obedience, in all the Members, in respect to every Matter susceptible of human direction, which forms the Cement of Union and binds the parts of Society together.[6] It is this only which can give to society a consistency of Laws, Regulation and Policy; which diffuses a similarity of Customs Habits and Manners, which fixes the national attachment and establishes an uniformity of Principle and Conduct and which leads them to act in concert, as one body, in all Matters where their Common Interest and Safety are concerned. And it is this Unity in the supreme power of Government which only can enable it to Collect and Command the whole strength of the several parts of the Society for its preservation and defence.[7]

A separation in Legislation gives us the most perfect Idea of two independent Societies. The only mark by which they are distinguishable is, the distinct obedience which their respective subjects pay to their several and respective supreme Heads. Two distinct and independent Powers in the same Society is the greatest of all Absurdities in politic Law. It is so contrary to reason, so inconsistent with the design of Civil Society, that it never was nor is to be found in any system of Civil polity, either Civilized or Barbarian in the World. They would be the never failing sources of perpetual opposition, discord, enmity and confusion

[5] This doctrine of the supreme will of the state as being vested in the legislative authority was apparently drawn by Galloway from Locke: *Candid Examination*, 10-11.

[6] In this whole paragraph, however, Galloway seems to depend more literally upon Jean Jacques Burlamaqui (1694-1748), *Principles of Natural and Politic Law*. He doubtless used the London edition of 1763; more than once he uses the phrase "in respect to every matter susceptible of human direction," which is Burlamaqui's phrase; *Candid Examination*, 12; Burlamaqui, *op. cit.*, II. 44-45: "The first characteristic [of sovereignty], and that from which all others flow, is its being a supreme and independent power, that is a power that judges in the last resort of *whatever is susceptible of human direction;* insomuch that this power acknowledges no other superior power on earth." Burlamaqui, of course, did not believe that this supreme, "independent" power was independent of the collective human will of society in its original establishment or creation; *op. cit.*, II. 23, 45.

[7] Cf. Burlamaqui, *op. cit.*, II. 22-31.

[134]

and subvert the very ends of Civil Society, which is an Union of Numbers for the purposes of their safety and happiness. "No Man can serve two Masters;" and "a Kingdom divided against itself can not stand."

A separation in legislation in respect to the objects of its power would be equally absurd and dangerous. The Affairs of Society subject to regulations are so interwoven together, so dependent on each other, that they cannot be separated without infinite mischiefs and confusion. Agriculture, Manufactures, Commerce and Taxes and the National safety are so many links of the same Chain and so dependent on each other, that to render them subservient to the purposes of Society they must be under one direction. Let us suppose that the regulation of each of these were under different supreme independent Powers, what would be the Consequences? Their regulations would often interfere and obstruct each other without a remedy.

And to grant an independent right, of raising Money and levying Taxes, to a part of a Society, is surrendering up the most essential right of the supreme Authority upon which its strength and safety depend. And, if it does not amount to a grant of absolute independence, it is at once furnishing the People with the means of becoming so.

Indeed it is a truth in which all Authors on Government agree, and which has been confirmed in the Systems of all Societies, that there must be one supreme legislative power, animated by one Will "which directs all its motions, and makes all its Members Act after a Constant and uniform manner to the same end, namely the public Utility.["][8] And that this power can admit of no division or sharing without destroying the harmony, and ultimately producing the ruin, of the Society.

In an absolute Monarchy this Unity of legislation is most simple because it is lodged in a single Person; It is less so in mixt or Compound Governments, where the Authority is placed in different Houses forming one body; and yet it is equally perfect,

[8] Burlamaqui, *op. cit.*, II. 26. The quotation is more correctly given in *Candid Examination*, 11. Burlamaqui's own words were: "Whereas the state is a body, or a society, animated by one only soul, which directs all its motions, and makes all its members act after a constant and uniform manner, with a view to one and the same end, namely, the public utility."

because the assent of all is made necessary to the validity of every Act. Upon a knowledge of the necessity of preserving this great principle in Civil Society the Romans acted when they abolished their first and established their second form of Government. Our Ancestors followed the example in their Union with Scotland and in giving a Representation in Parliament to Wales, Chester and Durham. And upon every principle of good Policy the American Colonies ought to be united in the same manner with Great Britain if it be possible. Because this Union is certainly the most perfect and will be therefore the most permanent.

If it was possible, that any other Arguments, save those which are evident from the beneficial effects of the precedents I have mentioned, are wanting to shew the propriety and advantage of this Union to both Countries, it is that arising from the distance of America from the Seat of Empire. The greater the distance, the greater is the necessity of a perfect Union. Because in proportion to the perfection of the Union will be the weight and influence of the State over its subjects in that distant Country. Indeed where this Union is perfect the distance of the Members from the seat of Empire makes little or no difference. Its laws and policy will equally pervade the whole System and like the powers of the human will, keep the extremities in the same Order and under the same Obedience and Subordination as it keeps the most contiguous Members.

It is a Notion which has been adopted of late, that the distance of the Colonies from the Seat of Empire renders it impossible to govern them. This opinion is founded in mistake. Whoever will rightly consider the nature of Government and its Operations, will find that the distance of a Member of the Politic Body has as little to do with the good or ill Government of it, or with its Obedience to the supreme Authority, as that of a Member of the human Body which, however distant or near, equally obeys the human Will. It is the Uniformity and Vigor in Government which constitutes and transmits its power equally through all the parts of Society, without regard to their locality in the Empire. And in proportion to these will be its subordination and obedience. Hence we have seen an Union with Scotland like a magical Charm, suddenly sooth incessant discontent and rebellion into

peace, order and just subordination, while the inferior politic
Members even at the feet of the supreme and executive Authorities of the State, through a want of that Uniformity are constantly
rising in opposition to the Measures of Government & throwing
its exertions into the greatest Confusion.

As to the practicability of obtaining the Assent of the two
Countries to this Union it cannot be determined until some essay
shall be made towards it. Various are the Sentiments of the
People on both sides of the Atlantic. It has never been proposed
and therefore not discussed in either. A few republicans in America, a very small part of the People, have condemned it, without
discussion and without ever consulting the People at large. They
would not permit it, with many other Matters of great Importance, to be discussed. And no one to this day can say whether
this Country will admit of it, however necessary it may be to the
safety and duration of the Empire.

Should the Plan before recommended take place it is further
proposed that all the regulations mentioned in the second, save
those that relate to the American legislature be added and make
a part of it.

A SECOND PLAN OF UNION & C.

If a Representation in Parliament cannot be obtained, from
objections arising on either side, then it is proposed that an
American Branch of the British Legislature be established in
America for the general purposes of American regulations only.
1st That this Branch consist of a perfect representation of the
Crown, an Upper House and a representation of the People. The
first to be appointed by the Crown; The Members of the second
to be appointed in like manner, vested with some degree of rank
or dignity above the Commons, and to hold their offices during
Life unless removed by the concurrent impeachment of the Kings
representative and the Lower House. And the Members of the
third to be chosen by the Assemblies of the several Colonies.
2nd That this Branch of Legislature be considered as an inferior
Branch of the British Legislature, united and incorporated with it
for the *general purposes* hereinafter mentioned. And that it be
established, that any of the said Regulations may originate and be

digested either in the Parliament of Great Britain, or in the American Branch; and being prepared transmitted, to the other for its approbation or dissent; and that the assent of both be requisite to the validity of all such regulations.

3ᵈ That the jurisdication of the American Branch be confined to such regulations as relate to the general police of the Colonies in which *Great Britain and the Colonies, the Colonies in General or more than one Colony* are concerned, as well civil and Criminal as Commercial.

4ᵗʰ That the Right of calling, prorogueing and adjourning, this Branch of the Legislature be in the Crown.

5ᵗʰ That each of the American Houses of Legislature, may with the Approbation of the Representative of the Crown, elect two Commissioners to sit in the two Houses of the British Parliament, with the Priviledges of the British Members, so far as relate to representing, and giving information of the Circumstances of their Constituents; But without any right to vote or decide upon the Question.

Remarks

1ˢᵗ If Unity in Legislation be absolutely necessary to the Union and safety of the Empire, and it cannot be procured by a representation in Parliament, there is no other mode of obtaining it ever yet invented, but by forming a new Branch and incorporating it with the Parliament, by mixing their jurisdictions together, and making the assent of both necessary to the Validity of their Acts. It is this joint assent that forms the Unity of Parliament and of all other mixt forms of Government. In some we find two, others three, four and five Branches thus incorporated. An increase in Number of Branches, is indeed, not desirable if it could be avoided. It renders the System less perfect and the Transaction of Business more dilatory and difficult. But these are difficulties which must give way to greater, and to necessity; and which perhaps in the present plan will be found less than in any other except in the one first proposed, when it is considered that the American jurisdiction is confined to the general Affairs of America only excluding the Provincial polity.

2ᵈ This Union will not be absolutely perfect, because the jurisdiction of the American House will not extend to the Affairs of Great Britain. These will remain the Objects of Parliamentary discussion and regulation; So that Great Britain will possess a Right, to interfere in all American Regulations; and a power, to prevent any of them from affecting her own Interest and Welfare, while America will be debarred from any interference with those which concern Great Britain or any other of its dominions; and yet it will effectually answer the two great purposes in View, of preserving the Rights of the Colonies and keeping them dependent Members of the parent State. No infringement of their Rights can take place without their assent, and by mixing the jurisdiction of their Branch with the British, no regulations beneficial or necessary to their interest and welfare can be adopted without the Consent of Parliament. The first will secure their Rights and the second their connection with, and dependence on, the principal State. Great Britain will possess an independent legislature of her own and hold an essential Share in that of America which will establish American Subordination.

3^d But Great Britain will have a further and very important Security for the dependence of America. The Crown will remain ever seated in Great Britain. Its powers, prerogatives and favors must all flow from thence; and yet will be equally extended to and prevail in America. All the executive Authority of the State, the rights of War and Peace, and of treaty with foreign Nations, the Right and Means of protection, the Military and Naval force, the strong Ports Forts and Garrisons in America, and all Appointments Civil and Military, Honorable, and Lucrative, will remain in its possession and flow from it; by which means a weight and influence will be established in America, Centering in Great Britain, so as to prevent any future attempt in the former to throw off her connection and dependence on the latter.

4th It may be objected that the Americans by this Plan will have sufficient Security for their Rights, but that the Crown will have no Certainty that the Aids will be granted when the wants and defence of the Empire require them. The Answer is, that there is more political and rational Security, that the aids will be granted under this Plan than in the mode of requisitions of the several Assemblies so often proposed, under a total exemption from

[139]

Parliamentary Taxation. This mode has been often tried, and its absurdity and impracticability proved by experience, at a time when parliamentary Authority was not disputed, nor intended so to be, but hung over the Colonies in Terrorem; and when they were in the most eminent danger of being conquered by a foreign Enemy, although every encouragement was given to allure them to the discharge of their equitable and necessary Duty. Some granted the aids required in one year, others in another, and some gave none during the War. Indeed this Conduct in the Colonies was to be expected, as the causes arose naturally out of that policy upon which their late connection with the principal State is founded. This mode may be tried again; but the same Causes will ever produce the same Effects, and the same if not greater delinquencies will be the result so that the present Plan cannot be worse but upon examination will be found to be better.

5th By this Plan the Causes of the Colonial failures in granting the necessary Aids will be removed. One arose from the disunited State of the Colonies and the want of any mode by which their just Quotas could be ascertained; another from the disputes between the proprietary Governors and their Assemblies respecting the taxation of the proprietary Estates and other Matters, a third from the local situation of the Colony it being remote from immediate danger and invasion by the Enemy; and the fourth arose from want of some general authority having jurisdiction *over the whole* to ascertain their respective Quotas and compel them to do their reasonable and necessary duty. Under the present Plan the Power of granting aids are placed in other hands, before whom none of those mischievous disputes or other obstructions can happen, and who are, besides made competent to the removal of all other difficulties.

6th It is in this plan a fundamental Stipulation and Condition of the Union, that whenever Great Britain shall give towards the national defence the Colonies shall give in a certain proportion. It is not to be presumed that the American branch will wantonly break the Stipulation as it is the great Base of the Union, Besides their Interest and Safety will teach them not to do it. The Enemies of Great Britain will be their Enemies. A war with her will be a War with them; and the Ground and Safety of their Happiness the same and not to be separated. They can give their Money into no other Hands but those of the Crown without a Convulsion in their Constitution which must destroy it; and if they refuse they must want its protection. To which must be added that in such Case the Parliament will have it in its power to refuse its assent to any beneficial Bills necessary to the Welfare and Interest of the Colonies. Thus all former disputes being adjusted and grounds of future discord excluded, mutual interest and safety will beget the desire of complying with this great and fundamental Covenant, and of preserving that union and Harmony which is so necessary to the Welfare and Happiness of both Countries.

7th The same Objection might be made to the Constitution of Parliament. It might be asked with equal reason, what Security has the Crown that the Commons will grant the necessary Aids? The only Answer is that it is their Interest so to do. And if they refuse they desert their own Safety; and must want that protection which was the great end of their entering into Society. This is all the Security the Crown can have in a mixt form of Government, and this it will possess under the Plan now proposed.

8th In order to preserve the same balance of Power between the Crown and the People in America as in Great Britain, and to give the Crown as representative of the whole legislature that Weight and Influence it has long wanted in America, it is necessary that the American branch of the legislature be established on the principles of a mixt Government. An entire democracy without the checks of Aristocracy and Monarchy would be dangerous to the State, an Aristocracy only would not form an union, but be too Arbitrary over the People and dangerous and ungovernable by the State. It will therefore be certainly best to blend the powers and Rights of all of them in the American branch in the same manner as they are blended in the principal State. These will ever be checks on the excess of Power in each other, and prevent their separation from the Principal Government, more especially when the Legislature of Great Britain is ever ready to throw its weight into the Scale where justice ought to preponderate. Besides it is of the utmost importance to the permanent Union of the parts of a great Empire that the same essential principles of Policy should pervade the whole System should run through every inferior and subordinate politic Body. There should be no deviation from those principles upon which the principal State is settled, be its form what it may. If it be Monarchial the Principles of Monarchy, If Aristocratical the principles of Aristocracy, If Democratical the Principles of Democracy, should be strictly adhered to in the forms of all the inferior Politic Bodies. And if it be a mixt form of Government then the principles of all of them should be so tempered and mixt together as to admit of no Variation from that Policy upon which the Principal State is established. In short every inferior Corporation or Body Politic should be *in Miniature* a perfect resemblance of the Principal Government and always subject to its controul and authority. Every deviation must destroy the balance and weaken the principal System. The principles of the different forms of Government are so opposite in their Natures that they can no more agree while independent and unmixed than fire and water. They may indeed be so blended together by Wisdom and Art as to moderate the violent effects and form a balance to each other, as a moist Atmosphere will cool a too heated Air and render it fit for respiration, but while they are independent of each other, or so injudiciously mixt as to give a superiority to one over the other, Weakness and Ruin must follow. It is this heterogeneous mixture of contrary principles not wisely tempered together which form a part of the Weakness of the British Government. Proofs of this truth might be adduced in the inferior Establishments within the Kingdom but the Proprietary and Charter Governments in America afford much stronger.[9]

THE PLAN CONTINUED

5th [*sic*][10] In time of War to prevent delay in granting extraordinary Aids to the Crown Bills for that purpose may be finally passed into Laws by the Kings representative being authorized by a temporary Act of Parliament.

6th The jurisdiction of the American branch being confined to the

[9] Cf. *Historical and Political Reflections*, 24-36; 123-24; *Plain Truth*, 41-42, 43, 44.

[10] The error in numbering the sections probably resulted from the fact that Galloway followed the Germain Plan of 1779, omitting to change the sequence when he inserted section 5 above.

general Affairs of America it will be necessary and perhaps good policy to give the Colonial Legislatures the Power of Regulating their own respective internal Affairs, subject as usual to the negative of the King in Council.

Remarks

The Multiplicy and variety of regulations, necessary to the Order and Welfare of the Colonies, would render the Business of Parliament, as well as of the American branch infinite; and it will be perhaps sound policy to confine the American Jurisdiction to general objects only without suffering it to intermeddle with the internal police of the several Colonies.

THE PLAN CONTINUED

7th The Peace establishment of each Country may be maintained by itself. In America perhaps best by the respective Colonies. But the Aids to be granted to the Crown by the American branch should be as the Wealth of one Country bears to the other. This proportion may be adjusted by a comparative view of the exports of both.

8th [sic] The proportion of each Country being settled it Should be a fundamental stipulation in the Compact of Union that whenever Great Britain shall give   America shall give

And so in proportion to any greater or less Sum given by Great Britain. And as the wealth of one Country may increase more than the other, it may be further stipulated, That when the exports of America shall rise or fall her proportion of Aids shall rise or fall in the same proportion.

9th [sic] The appointment of all Governors, Judicial, Ministerial, and executive Offices and Officers, as well those which concern the Administration of Justice as the collection, receiving and paying out the public Revenues and of all Military Officers, should be fixed in the Crown. In short the Prerogatives of the Crown should by no means be lessened or abridged by the Union, but remain the same in America as in Great Britain.

10th [sic] All acts of Assembly which affect the prerogatives of the Crown Should be repealed or annulled.*

* These Acts are already effectually abolished by the Institution of the New rebel States.

[143]

Remarks

There are many Acts of the Colonial Assemblies which take away the Prerogatives of the Crown and place them either in the hands of the Assemblies or the people at large such as the right of summoning, dissolving, Proroguing and adjourning Assemblies, and of appointing Treasurers, Sherriffs, Coroners, Collectors of the Public Revenue &c. &c. This weakens the Authority and influence of the Crown, and strengthens the Power of the People, so as to destroy that balance of Power which is the great Security of a Mixt form of Government.

THE PLAN CONTINUED

11ᵗʰ [*sic*] All the Governments of the several Colonies Should be reduced to one form and consist of a Governor and Privy Council to be appointed by the Crown and to hold their offices during pleasure. An upper House of the same Appointment whose Members Should hold their offices during good behaviour and to be removable on the joint address of the Governor and Assembly; and an Assembly chosen by the People.

Remarks

In applying an effectual Remedy to a disease we must examine into its Cause. The Seeds of the distempered State of America, as the Divines assert of Original Sin were planted in their original existence, in the formation of their political Societies. The fall from that perfection of mixt polity upon which the strength safety and freedom of the British Government was established, has involved the Government in all their present misfortunes. No care was taken in their original Charters to make an equitable provision for the exercise of the supreme Authority of the state over them. They were not represented in Parliament nor was any right granted them to be so. This was a Matter however important which neither the Crown nor the Emigrating Colonists seem to have attended to. The omission by the first was perhaps owing to the Arbitrary Policy of the times, and by the second to their inability to exercise the right. However when the Colonists arrived at a degree of Maturity which enabled them to exercise it, they found themselves totally excluded from, while the Free-

[144]

holders and landed Interest of Great Britain enjoyed their full participation of, it. They saw a parliament which had no Constitutional means of obtaining just information of their wants and necessities, and their true Circumstances making Laws to bind them. A parliament in which they were not represented and of course in which they had no Constitutional Opportunity of objecting to and reasoning against provisions made for their regulations, however mischievous to their true Interest and Safety. Hence upon looking up to the Principles upon which the English Constitution was established, and finding that every part of the realm enjoyed those Rights, they concluded that the British Government was both despotic and incompetent. Of this defect in the Colonial Institutions the Republican party made their advantage, and instead of leading the People to Petition for a right to be represented in Parliament, they led them into a rebellious opposition to Government.

But what has been more fertile in Mischief and more productive of the present disaffection in America to this Country is the Establishment of a Number of inferior Societies or Bodies politic on principles of polity utterly inconsistent with and repugnant to those of the principal State. In the New England Charters all the rights and prerogatives of the Crown, the supreme representative of the King Lords and Commons, were sacrificed to popular power. Not the least trace of either was reserved. Not only all the powers necessary to complete legislation, but all that relate to the administration of justice—to the Collection of the Public Revenue, the Appointment of all officers Civil and Military, and even to War and peace were granted to Persons who were to be elected by the People—Nor did the Crown in some of them even reserve a right to inspect their Laws or to enquire into their Conduct. Thus all the Rights of Monarchial and Aristocratical part of the English Constitution were omitted and perfect democracies established in these inferior Societies.

In the proprietary Charters all the Rights of Monarchy and the Prerogatives of the supreme representative of the King Lords and Commons were granted to private Subjects in Fee, in hereditary and alienable Tenure. The Legislative and executive authority of the State, and even the Rights of War and peace were given up

[145]

without the least check or controul reserved in the Crown over the Proprietaries their Governors, or the Officers they should appoint.

Every Civil establishment will have its influence on the Minds of the people over whom it is instituted. This influence will be led as the Principles of their Policy direct it. Men inured to a particular System of Government will be attached to it, and prefer it to all others. The Frenchman, Spainard, Portuguese or Turk will not change his System of Polity with a Briton. He loves his oppression and prefers it to true Liberty because he is used to it, and it has become second nature. The opposite of or that which materially varies from, what men love and admire they generally hate. Ought we then to be surprized when we find that the Seeds of Opposition and disaffection to the English Government thus early sowed in America should be now grown to some degree of maturity and that a part of the People, thus educated and instructed in a dislike to the principal State Should be fond of that independence which is so fully countenanced and inculcated by their Charters.

In truth, the general voice of all sensible Men in America impute the Rebellion to these Causes. They know it not from reason only but from experience. They have watched its rise and progress, and traced it from its causes to their Effects and from the Effects back to their Causes. They have seen it originate in the Charter and popular Governments of New England, and nursed and nourished in the proprietary. They have seen almost all the officers in the Charter Governments save those who held their offices and Salaries under the Crown, foremost and active in the Rebellion.

But further to convince them of the dangerous policy of instituting democratical power under a mixt Monarchy, they have seen a particular sect of religious People whose Principles naturally lead them to an admiration and love for Democracy, almost universally embrace the sedition against Government, & whose Ministers, even at the Altar, were the first to teach the People that the path of Rebellion was the high road to temporal as well as spiritual Happiness, while they saw but few of the Church of England and other Sectaries, except men of Bankrupt and des-

[146]

parate Fortunes, who did not oppose or refuse to be connected with a design so destructive of the Interest and Safety of both Countries as that of throwing off their subordination to the British State.

If these remarks are just, it seems very manifest that the Charter Governments require great Amendments and Alterations, if they are admissible on any ground of reason or Policy. The Democratical principles of the former never can accord with those of a mixt Monarchy. They destroy the Ballance of its power and never fail to produce factions and seditions against the principal State. Men educated under a popular form of Government and long indulged with excess of Liberty never can bear the necessary rigour of Monarchy or even of a mixt form of Government. They acquire prejudices in favor of the one they have lived under; believe it the best form and that their happiness can only be secured by it. And this creates an aversion to all others. Here habit becomes second Nature and cannot be eradicated but by contrary Customs and Practices and an abolition of the Policy under which their former Habits were obtained. This in the course of twenty years will root out the seeds of disaffection and rebellion in America, more especially as so much of the Old Attachment and Affection for the British Government remain among the People.

It has been observed before that it is of the utmost importance to the duration and strength of a great Empire that the same Principles of Government ["and Policy" deleted.—Ed.] should prevade all its inferior and subordinate Members. It is this identity of Policy that gives the same Spirit to the Laws and Creates the same mode of thinking and acting in the people and establishes the same customs, Manners, prejudices, Attachments and Habits throughout the Empire, so as to form as it were, one People of the same Mind, in respect to their subordination and obedience as well as to their own safety and happiness. It is the true source from whence Spring all national Attachments. This attachment we find even in the subjects of the worst and most Slavish forms of Government. What is it that induces a Frenchman, a Turk, the Slave of a Bashaw whose Life is at the disposal of His Master to prefer an existence under their Tyrants to all other forms of Government? It cannot be the Freedom they possess. It is the effects of certain policy and habits produced by it. They have been educated under and accustomed to oppression. That which would be intolerable to one not enured to it becomes by Habit easy to them, and not only tolerable but preferable, in Opinion, to that Liberty which is founded on different policy, Manners and Customs which they know not how to assume.

If this is the fact in Governments formed on Principles contrary to the rights of human Nature; if Men by Habit and Custom, may be taught to love misery and Slavery, how much stronger must their Affections and Attachments be when formed and fixed by that polity and those Habits and Customs which are coincident with the rights of Mankind and instead of Slavery secures their Liberty and Happiness?

The influence of this identity of the polity on the Peace and Harmony of Society is to be traced in all experience antient as well as modern. So long as Rome preserved its mixt policy upon which the Government was originally established it was powerful and invincible. Upon the Acquisition of Colonies and the establishment of a different system for their Government, a dispute arose founded in that dissimilarity of polity. The Empire was thrown into Confusion—The Social War took place, and the existence of Rome as an independent Society was endangered. But upon granting to the Colonists the Priviledges of Roman Citizens, of voting in the Comitia, and of being enrolled in the Legions &c.—They instantly returned to their Allegiance—The Enmity occasioned by the War was forgot, and the peace order and strength of the Empire restored. And afterwards had Rome adhered to its original mixt polity, and redressed with Justice the Grievances of the People, instead of suffering the Institution of the Tribunes, its mixt form of Government would have survived to a much longer period. But that unwise and unfortunate deviation from the original Principles of its Government, placed in a little time, these popular Officers above the Controul of the Senate and even of the Dictator himself. It destroyed the Balance of its power and brought on Commotions convulsions and finally death. So long as Scotland remained disunited from England in the same essential principles of Government, Jealousies, Enmities and War were the Consequences. But since the Union the seeds of discord and disaffection have been wasting into decay and Harmony and Peace have succeeded in their room. Had Chester Wales and Durham remained in their antient disfranchised State, in all probability they would now have been the Instruments of opposition to Government in the hands of the present faction. Had Ireland been included in the Union with Scotland we had not known the late dangerous Commotions in that Kingdom and had the principles of our mixt form of Government been originally settled in the Colonial Institutions and a Representation in Parliament been granted, it is beyond the degrees of probability, and scarcely within the confines of possibility that a Rebellion should have existed in America.

For the same reasons the Proprietary Governments ought to be changed into Royal. Long experience has proved that the exercise of the Prerogatives of the Crown ought not to be nor are they by Law grantable in Fee. They are not transferable at all. The Heir inheriting them may be either a weak or a bad Man. They are not in safe keeping in the Hands of the first and are dangerous Weapons in those of the last. Like a dark Cloud between the King and his People, they exclude the Rays of Royalty and prevent that respect and attachment which insures the obedience that every Subject ought to possess for his Sovereign.

The power of the Proprietaries are hereditary and were alienable before the Act of Parliament to prohibit it; or at least it was thought so; and being independent of the Crown they consider it as their own; and make use of it to serve the purposes of their own Ambition and Interest and forget that they hold it in trust for the honor of the Crown and the good of its People. If they surrender up the Prerogatives of the Crown to gratify the People, they not only receive the Rewards of Gratitude and Affection for it, but always a full compensation of Interest. If they make use of them to oppress and injure the subject the blame and odium falls upon the Crown. There are many instances where the most important Prerogatives of the Crown have been sacrificed to proprietary Interest and the Humour of the People. Insomuch that they scarcely know they have a Sovereign and never that they have a good one.

Nor would it be difficult to prove that the weight of Proprietary

[149]

power and Influence has been used against the Crown in the present Contest between Great Britain and the Colonies. And it will be found upon a Candid enquiry that the Prevalence of the Aristocratical as well as Democratical Principles of the Proprietary and of the Charter Governments in America has formed the great source from whence the present Rebellion has sprung. Had these Governments been originally formed upon the same Principles of mixt policy upon which the principal State is established, America had not known a Rebellion.

There is no Government in the Civilized part of the World except that of Great Britain, in which this identity of Policy is not adhered to and preserved. In all the Monarchies in Europe the principles of Monarchy, perfect and pure are not only established in the principal State but preserved in all the inferior and subordinate Corporations and political Societies. The same Uniformity of polity is to be seen in all the Aristocratical and Democratical Communities. By this means a similarity of Laws, Customs, Habits, Manners and Principles are universally dispersed, the national Attachment fixt, and the Order and Uniformity of the Society maintained. It is that policy which is gradual constant and impreceptable operations excludes all distinctions Jealousies and Opposition, establishes concord and harmony, and forms the great cement of Union, which binds the Members and parts of an Empire together.

If these Sentiments are just and Government does not intend to efface from the Minds of the Americans all Loyalty to their Sovereign, all respect for the Principal State, and all National Attachments, the Charter and Proprietary Governments must be abolished and all the inferior Systems of Colonial Polity fixt in those Principles upon which the British Government is established.

Nor can it be thought difficult when the present state of America and the disposition of the People towards it are considered, to carry this measure into Execution. The People of America very generally, a few interested Men in the proprietary and Charter Governments excepted would prefer the mixt polity of the Parent State to all others. The Assembly and People of Pennsylvania have long since petitioned for a change of their Proprietary for that of a Royal Government. They have prayed that the Crown

[150]

would fulfil the Contract made with the first proprietor for the purchase of it in the time of the late Queen by paying the residue of the Purchase Money. This Petition lies yet before his Majesty in Council undecided. And the People of Maryland from a Multiplicity of disputes arising from the Arbitrary conduct of the Proprietor founded in his Private Interest and equally inconsistent with the Service and Interest of the Crown and the welfare of the People are tired of that kind of Government. In the four New England Colonies, Men of Sense property and Influence have long since perceived and since the Rebellion more especially fully experienced the Evils and intolerable Oppression of their Democracies, Governments which has levelled all distinction between Men of the greatest Property and the lowest Poverty, which has effaced all respect to rank and dignity of Office and prostrated all obedience to Law and all Security of Property. Besides all the New England Charters are beyond all Controversy forfeited by the Rebellion. And those of the Proprietaries are not only forfeited but entirely abolished by the People and others established in their stead.* So that as soon as the force of the Rebellion shall be destroyed little more will be necessary than to propose and establish a New rational and judicious system in their places.

Having thus traced out the great outlines of a Civil Constitution between Great Britain and her Colonies which I am confident will nearly if not entirely agree with the wishes of the great bulk of the People of America, and which I apprehend will prove by far more lasting and permanent and more beneficial to Great Britain, thus any hitherto proposed, I will pass to the second Question of less difficulty. Viz^t. What Benefits and Priviledges in Commerce the Colonies ought to enjoy?

In the discussion and adjustment of this Question I imagine we shall meet with little or no obstruction or impediment, if we make reason and justice our Clues. For if the state shall have obtained in the Settlement of the Civil polity of the two Countries a reason-

---

* The New State of Pennsylvania have not only seized and confiscated all the Royalties, rights and privileges granted to the proprietaries by the Royal Grant of Cha. 2^d but all their property in that province, their located Manors excepted. An Estimate of the Value of that property is to be seen in the Appendix. [No Appendix is included in the manuscript.—Ed.]

able Security that the Colonies will in future maintain their peace establishment, will support the Officers of the Crown agreeably to their Rank and Dignity, and will grant their proportion of Aids towards the National defence, Great Britain can have in Justice no further pecuniary demands on them as Members of her Society. And while they thus perform all the Duties of perfect Members they will be intitled to all the Priviledges. No unjust or unnecessary distinction or difference should therefore be made between the Subjects in America and those in Great Britain, Scotland and Ireland, because these distinctions will ever prove the causes of Jealousies and discord and in the end cannot fail to produce a dissolution of their Union. And because it can be of no Consequence to the State whether a Subject grows rich by Commerce on the Ohio or in Cheapside while it can certainly command a just and reasonable proportion of his Wealth whenever necessary to the safety of the Society.

It is therefore proposed as an addition either to the first or second

PLAN

1st That the trade of the Colonies shall be navigated in the same manner and subject to the same regulations and restrictions as the Trade of Great Britain.

2^{d} That the Trade of the Colonies with foreign Nations shall be subject to the same regulations and restrictions, and liable to the same imposts and duties on every Article of foreign growth, produce and manufacture imported.

3^{d} That the Colonies shall have the same priviledges of exporting the Articles of their own growth and produce except such Articles as are necessary and wanting to support and carry on the Manufactures of Great Britain and to furnish its Navy with Naval Stores. And that these Articles shall be imported only into Great Britain.

4th That the Colonies shall not interfere in their Manufacturies with the Manufactures of Great Britain so as to trade with foreign Nations. Nor shall their Manufactures be exported to foreign Countries.

5th That upon these Principles and all others which shall be

ncessary to promote and secure the Commerce of the Nation the
Parliament shall have the sole right to superintend the Navigation
and Trade of America.

6th That all Acts of Parliament affecting the Colonies and inconsistent with the Principles of the Union when established be
repealed.

General Remarks

It has been apprehended and from that apprehension an Objection has arose to an American Union of the Colonies in a Legislative Body, that it will be dangerous to the Principal State, and
enable the Colonies to throw off their dependence. When this
Objection is considered it can have no Weight. We have seen the
Colonies already with little difficulty unite in a most dangerous
and independent Body the Congress, and Assume all the Legislative and executive Powers of Government. And should they return
to the same circumstances, they will certainly, at all times and
with equal ease, be able to repeat the same Conduct. We should
therefore endeavour to change those Circumstances for others
which may render an Union of the same dangerous Nature more
difficult, and if possible, impracticable. There is no other mode of
doing this but that of carrying over to the Colonies, that system
of mixt Polity, in which are contained the weight and checks of
Monarchial and Aristocratical powers against the excess of popular. This only can suppress democratical Intemperance, and reduce popular Influence within its just and constitutional bounds.
Nothing else, except Arbitrary and despotic Authority, which cannot be exercised in a mixt form of Government, can possibly answer the purpose. Besides it will certainly be more prudent to
suffer a general Assembly of the mixt kind, to meet occasionally at
the will and Pleasure of the supreme executive Authority of the
State, than an unconstitutional democratical and independent
Congress.—In the first case an excess of Power in the democratical
part will always be checked and suppressed by the Monarchial
and Aristocratical and Government whose Will and Resolutions
will be single and unembarrassed will have its weight and Influence in both the other Houses. But in the latter case, these Checks
will be totally wanting, and Government will be excluded from

[153]

all Opportunity of the least controul or Interference. Moreover, we may, upon very solid reason, expect, that when the Colonies shall have a constitutional Body, in which they are all represented, and to the Institution of which they have solemnly agreed, to look up to for general regulations, they will wish for or think of no other. A confidence in its Wisdom and Justice will take Place. They will be content with their decisions and not rebel.

And as to the danger that the American Branch thus united will break its Connection with Parliament. It is not to be presumed; indeed it seems scarcely within the degrees of political possibility. The variety of Checks, and of controuling and opposite Interests forbid it. For it cannot be supposed that the Representative of the Crown holding all his importance under it, and changeable at its pleasure, will unite in or not oppose the attempt. And it is equally improbable, that the Members of the Middle Branch which shall be composed of Men deriving all their Rank, Dignity, Power and Importance, from the Crown, and who will perfectly know, that, immediately upon a dissolution of the Connection, all their rights must fall a sacrifice to popular Confusion, and themselves be reduced from superior Eminence and Dignity in Life to a level with the populace, will not unite with the Crown in opposition to a Measure so ruinous to their own Interest and Safety. This Objection therefore is not founded in Reason. It is opposed by the nature of the establishment. But was it otherwise; the apprehended Consequence of this Union, cannot take place, but from a Variety of Causes uniting to effect it, which must be visible and known, and which cannot be produced of a sudden. And we may safely conclude that Government more attentive to and watchful over the Conduct of the Colonies than heretofore, and availing itself of former omissions and experience will suppress such a design in the Bud, or at least before it arrives at a dangerous maturity.

Should the Military force of the Congress be once reduced, their Civil Authority and that of every inferior state will fall of course, and the Old forms of Government being destroyed by the Peoples own Act as well as forfeited by the rebellion, the whole Country will be in a state of Nature without a Civil Constitution— A perfect blank—until a new policy shall be established. And upon a view of the present parties in America it will be found perhaps more easy to constitute a new system of Government than to restore the Old. These circumstances prevent the most favorable opportunity of establishing such a general system of Civil Authority, as well as of inferior and subordinate Governments, as shall be best calculated to preserve and perpetuate the Union between the two Countries.

America is now divided into two parties, one of whom nothing else will satisfy than perfect Independence, because they are actuated by views of Ambition and Private Interest; The other, who ardently wish for a perpetual Union between Great Britain and the Colonies, upon Principles of Liberty and sound Policy, from a Conviction that their own safety and happiness depend upon it. The one is a mere republican party firmly attached to democratical Government, and have therefore vested the Powers of all their new States originally and ultimately in the People. The other as firmly attached to a mixt form of Government which equally guard against the abuse of power in the Sovereign & the licentiousness of the People. And altho' the party first mentioned by a variety of adventitious and favorable Circumstances, has been enabled to assume the Power over the other, yet as the last contains a very great Majority of the Men of Property and of the Colonists in general, who being secluded from all share in the Government and having suffered in the extreme under a Power in which they have no participation, would willingly embrace any proposals which afford a rational prospect of relieving them from their distress and ensuring future liberty and safety.

Upon this brief state of American parties, it will certainly be the best policy to propose and adopt that system of Civil Government which is most agreeable to the People, and promises the most lasting Union between the two Countries—Whether the prejudices of the Colonists against a representation in Parliament may not be so fixt as not to be removed, upon a fair and full discussion, is uncertain.* But should this be the case the Colonists have imbibed no prejudices against an American legislature incorporated with the Parliament. Many Men of the best Under-

* However the uncertainty of success, in a matter of so much Importance, and where a failure cannot be mischievous, shou'd not discourage the attempt.

standing, Weight and influence in the Colonies wish it had been adopted by the Congress when proposed, and even a Majority of that Body before they had fixt their resolution to be independent publickly approved of and supported it.

The grand foundation of the Union being settled the other Articles of lesser Consequence to America will be easily adjusted, especially if the Resolution of Government be to extend the same measure of Power and Freedom to the Colonies as in Great Britain. There will be Principles fixt and unalterable to refer to, in case of Objection and Dispute. The Prerogatives of the Crown, the Rights of the Subject, and the Balance which holds the Security of both, are well defined and ascertained in the Constitution of the English Government. These may and ought to be made the Test of decision. To this Test the Americans can have no just Objections nor hold any Argument against it, because an extension of those Principles to America is the only means of giving them the same Liberties that are enjoyed by their fellow Subjects in Great Britain, and of establishing a permanent security for their Freedom in a lasting Union between the two Countries.

In communicating these sentiments, I have endeavoured to trace the subject from its first principles, to state facts and remove objections that your better judgement may avail itself of whatever of them, you may think right. I know I have been prolix, and I fear unmethodical and inaccurate; but the Importance of the subject and the little time I have been able to employ on it, with your favourable opinion of my Intentions, will plead an excuse for those defects.

I have the honor to be with the most perfect Respect, Sir,

Your most obedient and
most humble Servant
J. GALLOWAY

The right Honorable
CHARLES JENKINSON, ESQUIRE, &c. &c.

PLAN OF UNION *ca.* 1785[1]

FEW MEN, I fear, propose anything in favour of government with a view entirely abstracted, from private interest. And certainly, when such a suspicion prevails, it must throw a disagreeable shade over the offered plan. To prevent therefore all imputations of that kind, I, on honor, do solemnly declare, that I have not a desire for any employment under government. Because, for several reasons, I am persuaded, that it is not in my power, to fill any office with a degree of ardour and reputation at all proportionate to my wishes. My only request now is that His Majesty may suffer an old and faithfull officer, tho nearly ruined by his uniform and constant attachment to his Majesty's government to retire on what, considering his former style of life & services can not be deemed extravagant.

In order to found a permanent and happy constitution in his Majesty's colonies on the Continent of America, I conceive it necessary to give one general form of government to all such as are or may be settled by natural born british subjects. Such an establishment will prevent that confusion, which must result from different systems; especially in places contiguous to each other, and inhabited by such subjects. The people now in contemplation are such, and by birth entitled to all the rights and privileges of Englishmen. Therefore the form of government in such british colonies ought to be as similar to the constitution of Great Britain as the distance of the countries, and the difference between a parent State and colonies will admit.

This grand and important object justly merits the most accurate attention, as well as the most serious exertions of men of the first abilities and purest principles. Radical errors, in all cases, must prove destructive. And particularly so in rules formed for the

[1] The original manuscript of this document is in the Division of Manuscripts, Library of Congress. It is a rough draft, filled with corrections, interlinear additions, etc. For the sake of clarity, the basic, or original text, has been followed.

regular and proper government of societies. If error is originally admitted into the plan, it will be found more difficult to remedy, and will produce a greater variety of evils than anyone can readily point out. And as it is scarce possible materially to alter the public constitutions of any people; especially an informed and free one, without imminently endangering the safety and happiness of the whole community, the greatest care ought to be used in the original formation of a government or constitution for subjects of that description.

I am very conscious, that it is far beyond my present abilities to give a complete draft of the desirable and necessary plan. So complexed is the nature, and so extensive and interesting are the consequences of it, that none should attempt it but such as have their heads and hearts more entire and more at ease than I can boast of. Therefore my only attempt will be to give some general hints on the subject, in the order they occur to my mind, and leave such to be properly arranged and corrected by some masterly hand. In doing even this, my want of every book necessary to assist my memory, and inform my judgment, will abridge my observations.

In governmental concerns many difficulties have arose in America. But nothing contributed to their existence so much as the distance of that country from Great Britain. Too often, before proper information could be given to, and instructions received from the latter, such have swelled into real evils. Sometimes local circumstances shifted so suddenly and violently between the giving information, and receiving instructions how to act, as entirely to change the immediate and proper objects of attention. So that Government could not avoid proceeding on erroneous principles in the application of a remedy. And too frequently an immediate one, which could not constitutionally be procured till government afforded it, was indispensibly necessary to stop disorders in the body politic. The great lapse of time before it could be obtained gave full scope for such disorders to encrease and rage so universally; as to render the intended remedy ineffective. The late rebellion affords many melancholly instances in support of the above remarks.

To guard against, as much as possible, such dangers in future,

[158]

no better method, probably, can be suggested than the appointment of a Lord Lieu[t] or Gov[r] Gen[l] over the whole of such colonies, with a Council of   persons, duly qualified for the trust, on which every thing depends, under the style of privy counsellors, or any other which may be thought proper. His Lordship to be president. And a certain number, which must be proportioned according to the whole, to make a board. This president and Council to be invested not only with ample general powers in America, but expressly with the following:

First, to convene before them all or any of the provincial Governors, either to procure information of the general or particular state of all or any one of the colonies.

Secondly, on any sudden emergency, officially to advise, or order such Gov[rs] how to act. And to render that power effectual, express instructions should be given to such Governors, in all such cases, immediately to inform the said President and Council thereof, and to obey their advice or peremptory orders thereon.

Thirdly, on the mal-conduct of any such Governor, the s[d] Govr Gen[l] to be impowered either to reprimand or suspend him from his office; as the case may require. And if the latter, only untill his Majesty's pleasure can be known. And to appoint some proper person to succeed him in the interim. In all instances of suspension, the person deprived of his office to have, in writing, and under the hand and seal of the said President, the reasons for it, within   from the day of the suspension.

Fourthly, the President and Council, and in case of the non-concurrence of the latter with the former, the President alone, to have the power of commanding the assistance, and directing the actual service of the military, within such colonies, both by land and by sea, in cases of imminent danger and popular insurrections. For which purpose they should be clothed expressly with sufficient civil authority. And at all times of fortifying where, and in such manner as they shall think fit, subject only to his Majesty's controul, and making full recompence for any private property that may be damaged thereby.

Fifthly, to reduce the medium of all such british colonies to one general standard.

And lastly, to have a superintending power over all laws, both temporary and perpetual, to be made in and by any of the legislative courts in the colonies aforesaid. And before any such law shall be in force to approbate the same. For which end each colony should be obliged to cause such laws to be laid before the said President and Council, who, within a given time, should also be obliged, under their or a majority of their hands and seal of their board, either to approve or negative the same and to give due notice thereof to the Governor and Council of such Colony. But in case of the latter, such colony to have the right of sending the same to his Majesty for his inspection and royal approbation, which if granted, such law should be in full force notwithstanding the negative of the Ld Lieu^t and his Council.°

This Council ought to be commissioned *quamdiu se bene gesserint*. The reasons for this opinion are many. It should be recollected, that as the institution will be new, the inhabitants of Nova Scotia; especially those who have been educated and lived in the several ceded colonies in America, exempt from any such power, even from long habit, the parent of prejudice, may be jealous of it. In many, a suspicion grounded even on that passion, may prove too strong to be removed by reason. This will either sink their spirits, and of course prevent their exertions in forwarding the rise of the settlement, or inflame their passions to a degree which finally may prove extremely prejudicial to it, as well as fatal to the mother country.

Nothing can have so great a tendency to reconcile men, of the above descriptions to the measure, as forming it on the most generous and candid basis. But nothing can command such a sincere and ready submission to any decision of the said board, as the knowledge of their independency. This reason is founded principally on policy. But if the proposition is considered in a more abstracted light, I conceive, it will be found in that view of it, to stand on solid truth. The appearance of any jealousy in the parent state over her colonies, if without foundation, will be too much for the spirit of virtuous and valuable english subjects long

° Note. Real mischiefs have arose from the ill wording of some of the former American charters, touching the royal sanction to colony laws. By said charters such laws were in force *from* their being enacted, and until dissented to by his Majesty. That certainly gave some time for their operation without the royal sanction, and which, for obvious reasons, ought not to have been granted.

to bear. And if such jealousy, in some degree, should be justifiable, it will serve the factious as a most dangerous weapon against government, and to lessen the ardor of the more cool and better disposed, in favour of it. Reason certainly dictates that in all free governments, whenever trustees are appointed for the reciprocal happiness of the Sovereign and the subjects, such should be placed on the surest and most liberal footing, which the subordination necessary in all States will admit. A deference for, and obedience to the Ministers of government, and their acts, are the only true and durable cements of society; therefore, whatever best cultivates and ensures those indispensible requisites, must ultimately prove the best calculated and most effectual for the interest of all parties. Many other observations naturally offer on this subject. But to proceed further into it would be exceeding the limits I have set myself. And I hope a misappropriation of time.

The internal police of the said board must be founded with the creation of it. And to complete the designed utility thereof, the political existence of the members ought to be strongly secured. Nothing can more effectually do that than rendering them safe from any unreasonable or unjust exercise of power by the President. Yet they should not be left too independent of him. Perhaps some rules similar to the following may answer the above purposes. The other will naturally be contained in their instructions.

His Majesty positively to order the President to consult and advise with his Council on all the laws to be formed in the colonies, and in all other matters of consequence. In all of less moment to leave him to his discretion. But he should not be bound to follow their advice; yet should expressly be made responsible for all consequences which may result from neglecting, in great concerns, or acting contrary to it. In case of the death, or absence of the President the eldest Counsellor to preside, but without the power of suspending governors.

If any of the members of the said Council should die, resign, or without leave from his Majesty, or the president under his hand and seal of office absent themselves for the space of   days from their duty, unless such absence should be occasioned by sickness or unfortunate accident; then the President to be impowered to suspend such delinquents during his Majesty's pleasure, and name others to fill their places, who, after qualifying themselves, shall act as members till the royal pleasure is known. The President also to have the same power of suspension in all instances of mal-feazance in office of the said members. But in both instances under the same rule of notice, and reasons as before directed as to governors. Qu: If such suspension should finally be adjudged vexatious or unjustifiable by his Majesty in Council, should not the President, in such cases, by an express Act of Parliament, or otherwise be made liable to an action at law for the recovery of damages by the injured party?

(Note) It may be thought doubtfull whether such an institution can constitutionally proceed merely from his Majesty. To obviate that difficulty, two methods propose themselves. First, an Act of Parliament for the purpose. And secondly, a charter confirmed by Parliament declaring the same. The latter appears to me as safe as the former, and perhaps will be less exceptionable. Such President and Counsellors should be specially protected in their persons and characters by an Act. And among the officers of the said board, none can be more necessary than a very candid and able solicitor.

All officers civil and military, Heads of Colledges, and other public seminaries of learning, all Fellows of the same, Barristers and Attorneys, before they shall be duly qualified to act in their several departments, and all students before they shall be entitled to their degrees, should take the State Oaths, as well as the oath of offices or profession where any such shall be appointed. But the form thereof should be enlarged by inserting a clause of true and faithful obedience to the british parliament, and such laws, as they shall from time to time make *expressly* relative to the british colonies in America: excepting only laws of taxation either of real or personal property in America. But the power of Parliament to regulate trade in that country, by levying such duties from, or entirely prohibiting such parts of it, as from time to time, they shall think fit, must be acknowledged and recognized by such officers and others in as strong terms as the English language can furnish. The same oath should be taken by all members of all legislative Courts, and officers of all other courts in his Majesty's American dominions aforesaid.

[162]

Legislative Courts there must be, or the English constitution will be annihilated. If that grand basis is destroyed all lesser dependent parts of it will fall of course. But care ought to be taken to remedy an evil which existed under the charters heretofore granted to several of the United States in America. In some of which for example the Massachusetts, every town consisting, if I recollect right, of forty freeholders, might elect and send a member to the General Court. Several had a right to send two, and Boston four. This was an impolitic indulgence; and therefore should not again be granted. As new settlements can not admit of a number of counties sufficient to form out of the same a proper legislative representation of the whole people, there remains no other alternative but making up that constitutional body from the several towns in each county. In forming a regulation on that plan, I am of opinion, that the number of freeholders in each town, necessary to acquire a right of sending a member to assist in legislation, should be encreased above forty. And to avoid placing the freeholders and others in towns not consisting of a sufficient number, but duly qualified to vote, on a disagreeable footing, that such should be deemed legal voters in the nearest adjacent qualified town. No person to be qualified to be a member of the house of Representatives unless actual seized in fee of a real estate in the colony of the value of It must not be large, as the inhabitants of that country in general can not be proprietors of real property of much value. Or possessed of a net income of   annually arising from personal property. (But quaere as to this.) The qualification of voters ought to be cautiously attended to, and accurately ascertained. If the choice of members should be triennial, two good consequences, at least, would, I apprehend, result therefrom. The assembling the people annually for the election of Representatives often occasions cabals and disorders, which, by that mode, will in part be prevented. And secondly, it will render the members independent, in a proper degree, of the people; and consequently induce them to act with more freedom and firmness in the due support of government.

What was called the residentiary Act in his Majesty's late American colonies produced, I really believe, more mischief than good. Therefore I conclude it best to suffer the Voters to choose their Representatives from the people at large qualified as aforesaid. Confining the choice to Residents in the towns certainly limits it. And in remote new settlements, though there may be a sufficient number of freeholders to send a member, on trial it will be found, in most instances, that characters, fit for that trust, will not be to be mett with among them. Men whose advantages in education have been but slender, and whose seclusion from the great and busy body of the people almost uninterrupted are naturally led into narrow, and sometimes illiberal notions of complexed and grand objects. Such persons for the want of more extended ideas than they commonly possess, seldom can comprehend the whole scope of government in all its interwoven and dependent parts, or the intimate connection and necessary unity of the whole. But rather think it their duty to study and partially promote the immediate interest of that part which they represent without duly weighing what effect any proposed measure may have on the whole political body.

Whether this, or any other plan for the formation of legislative bodies in the American colonies, be adopted, it will certainly be the most prudent, because the most safe mode, to have it explicitly marked out in the charter of the same. In short, all the fundamental corporative rights which the people are to enjoy should have a coexistence.

(Note) The larger bodies of men are, the more false importance they reflect on each other. That importance does not add to their understanding, but rather renders them vain and refractory. By lessening the number of Representatives the expence of them will be diminished. And business will be sooner dispatched. And lastly it will lessen the number of fools and knaves often too abundant in such assemblies.

Instead of his Majesty granting each government, consisting of natural born subjects, a charter. Quaere, if it would not be more safe to enact one general Act of Parliament, to be called and to operate as the Magna Charta of such subjects, comprehending all, which might be contained in such charters relative to the mere rights and privileges of the people? As this may be thought an infringement on the royal prerogatives, I will not venture an opinion on it. However, if such charters shall originally proceed from his Majesty, may not an Act confirming certain essential parts thereof pass? I apprehend that valuable consequences will flow from it. On the one hand, the Americans have held, and possibly may again hold, that charters are compacts between the King and them. And that Parliament, not being a party, have not any cognizance of, or jurisdiction over those compacts, consequently can neither abridge, or enlarge the same. On the other, Parliament have claimed and exercised the right of doing the first, which includes a like power as to the last. The above method will settle that most dangerous dispute, by connecting the American constitutions expressly with the authority of Parliament. I do not mean that such an Act shall be any legal bar to proceeding, if necessary, in the ordinary course of the law to vacate such charters for the non-user or mis-user thereof.

The Counsellors in each province to be appointed by his Majesty agreeable to the late institution in the Massachusetts. The neglect of this measure in the founding of that province, and the public evils resulting therefrom, sufficiently evince the necessity of it; as well for the interest of the people as of the King. Such should be under the power of the Govr so far as relates to suspension, which should remain in force till his Majesty's will thereon can be known: unless such suspension should be revoked by the Lord Lieu^t by the advice of a majority of his Council, to whom the party suspended should have a right to apply for redress. But the Governor should be obliged, in writing under his hand, and the seal of the province, to give his reasons therefor to the suspended person within   days from such suspension. Nor should any charges, but such as may be contained in the said writing be admissible either before the King in Council or the Lord Lieu^t and Council, to criminate the accused party. No pay from the Crown shd be allowed Councellors.

In all cases, according to the genius of the English laws and constitution, every person charged with criminality, must be put on fair ground, by having his crime specifically mentioned in the indictment, to which alone the trial must be confined. And he also has a right to know the charges alledged against him. Or in other words, what he is to answer for, a convenient time before his

[165]

trial, in order properly to defend himself. In both which instances the said laws and constitution are indisputably founded in reason and justice. If such charges should prove false, and to proceed rather from private resentment, or sinister views than public virtue, no good reason can be assigned why the innocent should not be protected, and the guilty made liable to answer the former in damages by some express provision for that purpose. But on the contrary it will give a freedom of acting to those who constitutionally ought to·possess it.

The appointment of all Judges of the highest executive Courts ought as well as the first judge of the common pleas & the paymt of them to rest in the King. And to which there cannot be found a reasonable objection, if such are commissioned *quamdiu se bene gesserint*. On a candid and correct examination of that mode, I am convinced, that it will be found very advantageous to his Majesty's real interest. Many reasons may be assigned for that opinion, but I shall mention only a few. First, it is what all the sensible friends of government in America most earnestly wish. And therefore it will be, among such, universally gratefull. Secondly, the administration of justice should be as free from *even* a suspicion of biass, fear, or partiality as possible. Because that adds the greatest weight and consequence to legal decisions, which are indispensibly necessary for the support of regular government. Thirdly, it will take off the dangerous distinction heretofore used to the worst of purposes between the independency of a judge in England, and the dependency of one in America. And lastly, it will convince his Majesty's American subjects, as well as others who, in future, may be inclined to become such, that he is as much attached to their interests and rights, as to his british. The happy consequences of which are too obvious, as well as too numerous to be mentioned.

I am sensible objections may be stated to this mode, but am confident such may be easily obviated. In short, I esteem the creation of Judges during pleasure a political absurdity. Because by such appointments the very end of the institution, in a great degree, is frustrated, by lessening the public confidence essentially necessary to support such officers. The necessity of courts of justice in all communities will not be denied. To found therefore such on a plan that will best answer that necessity, of consequence, must be acting prudently.

(Note) I do not choose particularly to disclose the inconveniences of judges being annually chosen by the people, as was the practice in some of the late colonies, or appointed by the Governor, with the approbation of the Council, as was the mode in others. Because such remarks may be applied to persons now in being. But as I have been very conversant with Courts in America, shall only generally say, that it is my firm opinion, real mischeifs did and will exist under both those modes. The salaries ought to be ample to induce Gentlemen of the first abilities and integrity in the law line, for of such they ought to consist, to quit their practice for seats on the bench. This will ensure, as well as is possible, a respectable Bench and a reputable bar. Many and great difficulties have arose in the late American colonies by the appointment of very different descriptions of men to such offices. An able and a confidential Attorney and Sollicitor General will be absolutely necessary, nor less so a similar Advocate General.

It must be of the utmost consequence that proper jurors should be returned to serve in the common law courts. The method of choosing such therefore must also be of real importance. Generally the one observed in England is deemed the most eligible. Yet it must be conceded that in London the people elect the Sheriff. But in most parts of America that officer is appointed virtually by the Governor, who, in all royal governments, is nominated by the King. From which difference originated the dislike of the colonists to jurors being returned *ad libitum* by the sheriff. A mode probably may be pointed out which, in a great measure, will ease the difficulty, by satisfying the minds of his Majesty's loyal American subjects, without endangering his interest. The point by them is justly deemed to be very interesting.

It hath been too customary for the General Courts in the eastern colonies to interpose an authority, rather subversive of justice than in support of it, of granting new trials. This practice too often hath been attended with shocking consequences, and always will be liable to the same. It ought therefore to be abolished. The judges are the persons with whom the law hath wisely placed that power. And they only ought to exercise it.

[167]

(Note) On trial it will be found sound policy to keep the legislative and executive powers as much detached from each other as the nature of government will permit.

In some of the late colonies, from trials by juries, appeals, which are merely civil law institutions, did lye to the King in Council, both in real and personal actions. In others only in personal. The impropriety resulting from a certain known rule of law of his Majesty in Council taking cognizance by appeal of actions tried by a jury of the vicinity, especially real ones, in which there may be a view, is not to be avoided and that rule preserved entire. Nor can certain mischeifs, which may arise, be guarded against, if such appeals are not granted. In fact, this is one of the instances in which the strict rules of law, as applied to the colonies, operate against the safety of the mother-country. And the only question is, whether the preserving the rule in full force as the right of the people, or controuling its operation to prevent public danger shall have the preference. I am of opinion, that it will be most eligible to allow appeals under certain conditions and regulations in both actions; but certainly in personal ones. If in real, it shall be where the demanded premisses shall amount to   in value to be ascertained, in case of a doubt, by persons under oath to be appointed by the court for that purpose. And in personal where the damages demanded are   or more. In these latter actions, even if the damages demanded are less than that sum, it should still be discretionary with the judges, provided the damages recovered shall amount to   to grant such appeals. Because if any certain sum is fixed, the damages will be laid under it, perhaps a shilling, or some other trifling sum, purely to prevent an appeal. This is no uncommon artifice. And because such a discretionary power may greatly check vexatious suits against Crown officers, and others of certain principles. In case the plaintiff, or any responsible person for him, will recognize in court, with two sufficient sureties, to restore the sum recovered with full costs, if the judgment shall be reversed on the appeal, no *cessat executio* to be granted. The appellants necessary costs frequently amount to sixty or seventy pounds. And yet sometimes he can not on a reversal get more than seven or eight taxed. This is a very great hardship on the innocent and much in favour of the guilty; and therefore requires a remedy.

(Note) Probably these will require some regulations touching what shall be deemed legal evidence before the King in Council, if appeals are allowed.

If ever there was any true policy in erecting a board of Commissioners of the customs in North America, it must have arisen from the extensive dominions which his Majesty then held in that country, And which reason now is no more. Therefore the expence of such Commissioners, with their unnecessary train of officers, may be saved. A Surveyor General of the Customs probably may soon be wanted.

It is indispensibly necessary both for maritime matters, the preservation of the laws of trade, and Mast Acts, that an Admiralty Court should be in every colony, with the usual jurisdiction thereto belonging. Because in the two last instances it will be, probably, very difficult to find impartial juries to try prosecutions founded thereon. The first speaks for itself.

Some explicit laws touching the Court of Admiralty are necessary rather to obviate ill founded objections than to settle the law. It has been disputed, whether the Keepers of the county prisons are, by law, obliged to receive prisoners sent them by a process from that court. To take away all pretence of dispute on that head, it may be settled by the charter or an Act. There has also been a difficulty touching the right such judges had of holding their Courts in the County Courthouses. That therefore ought to be settled in a similar manner. The fees of that court, as well as those of the custom house officers, ought to be settled by Parliament, and not left to the provincial assemblies. But neither ought to be high.

(In founding all governments, it is true policy to remove every cause of dispute and litigation; especially all such as may involve the Officers of the Crown.)

As town meetings have been the sources of much evil, and as such meetings must be, it is necessary, that the same should be expressly confined within the proper limits. I know of no method more adequate to the necessity than pointing out in the most explicit and definitive terms, for what purposes such shall be called, and when and where held. The regulations to extend expressly to adjournments of such meetings, as well as to their opening. Latterly under the word "Prudentials" used in some provincial acts for the regulation of town meetings, particularly in Boston, the voters assumed legislative and other powers never intended to be vested in them. Therefore no such general term ought to be used in the institution of such assemblies—but every object within y^r cognizance ought expressly to be marked ought.

In such meetings the people have knowingly exceeded their authority, though in consequence thereof they wilfully exposed themselves to a law-process for so doing; yet the remedy not being as sudden as the mischeif, the latter was effected. Therefore Q: whether it will be improper, in cases of necessity, to give the Governor or Commander in Chief with the advice of Council for the time being, express authority, by force if required, to disperse such assemblies when they clearly assume an excess of power, and of course become unlawfull? This point I confess to be very delicate; yet it is very interesting to government. If this method sh^d be thought too harsh, another offers, i.e. by Statute or by the Charter to render null & void all votes, acts & business of such meetings if in any one instance they exceed their power. This must be confessed not so effective a mode as the former.

In all colledges and other public seminaries of learning Caution ought to be used to prevent the principal trusts being lodged in the hands of gentlemen whose religious tenets point them decidedly to republicanism. The heads of all societies have a great influence over the youth belonging to the same. A slight retrospection of the late conduct in America will not only substantiate this observation, but evince the danger hereby intended to be avoided. However I would not be understood as aiming at any illiberal distinction between different opinions among protestants. For certainly I detest all degrees of persecution in all systems.

The ports for entering and clearing vessels should be as few as possible, consistent with the nature and convenience of the trade of the colony. For in such, distant from the Metropolis, it is next to impossible to prevent smuggling. Sometimes the under officers, so situated, have not force enough for that purpose. But oftener, being at a distance from their Superiours, are, for obvious reasons, inattentive or something worse.

All fortresses to be garrisoned by the King's troops, which must be under the command of the Lord Lieu'. No ships of war to be built, or employed by the Colonists without his permission in writing under his hand and seal of office.

All the Acts of trade relative to the colonies ought to be very carefull revised, in some instances corrected, in others repealed, and collected into one seperate code. At present they are too much blended with Acts respecting Great Britain and Ireland. This naturally creates confusion, and consequently difficulties in the construction of the first mentioned acts.

The masts Acts in a very special manner require attention. And I am persuaded an entire alteration. Every appointm' which is to be vested in his Maj' ought to be expressly reserved to him in the charter.

The vacant Crown lands in America ought to be managed with the utmost prudence both for the preservation of masts, and settlement of the same with people, I mean protestants, attached to the british constitution and government. Nor ought those lands to be granted to any person in very large quantities; for such grants are public evils.

The within mentioned general heads include a numerous variety of particulars. To collect and methodize which will prove a very arduous task and engross much time. A minute and accurate inspection of the laws and charters, especially the last, of the late colonies, and a knowledge, founded on experience, of what has occurred under the same, as well as a competent knowledge of the british constitution will, I humbly conceive, be found necessary to complete the important business. But as those particulars are not intended to be the subjects of the present enquiry, I shall leave the same to other gentlemen much better qualified for so large and interesting a business than I *ever* was. And only add *Non sum qualis eram.*

It may be objected that this plan is attended with many and great difficulties, and much labour. I own the charge to be true:

[171]

but must also remark, that the only proper time for setling a regular and wise constitution for his Majesty's American colonies is the present. And that delays will not lessen but add to and encrease such difficulties. And lastly, that the vast importance of the object to be obtained, if judiciously conducted, must infinitely outweigh every other consideration.

PLAN FOR A PERMANENT UNION
1788[1]

A PLAN for facilitating the reduction of the Revolted Colonies, and for establishing a permanent UNION between them and Great Britain.

That Commissioners be appointed, one of the Military profession, and two well acquainted with the principles of the British Constitution with powers to superintend, and direct the seizing upon and disarming the disaffected and rebellious, to embody the Loyalists in Arms, for the defence of their several Colonies, to receive the submission of the people to Government, and to direct the taking of the Oaths of Allegiance to the Crown.

That a proclamation be issued offering a general Pardon with proper exceptions, to all persons in Rebellion who shall, within—
days after the King's forces enter a Colony, bring in their Arms, and take the Oaths of Allegiance to Government; and that a tender of the following plan of Union be made to the People.

That a fourth branch of the British Legislature be established in America, for the purposes of American regulations only.

That this branch consist of a perfect representation of the Crown in the Character of a LORD LIEUTENANT, an upper House, and a representation of the PEOPLE. The first to be appointed by the Crown, and to hold his Commission during it's pleasure—The Members of the Second to be appointed in the like manner, and vested with the title of Baron, or some rank above the Commons, and the Members of the Third to be chosen by the Assemblies of the several Colonies.

That this branch of Legislature, be considered as an inferior branch of the British Legislature, united and incorporated with it, for the general purposes hereinafter mentioned. And that it be established, that any of the regulations to which it is made competent, may Originate and be digested either in the PARLIAMENT of

[1] Original in the possession of Lawrence J. Morris, Esq., of Philadelphia.

GREAT BRITAIN, or in the American branch, and being prepared, it may be transmitted to the other for approbation or dissent; and that the Assent of both be requisite to the validity of all such Regulations.

That the Jurisdiction of the American branch be confined to such regulations as relate to the general police of the Colonies, in which Great Britain and the Colonies, the Colonies in general, or more than one Colony shall be concerned, as well Civil and Criminal as Commercial.

That the right of calling proroguing and adjourning this branch of the Legislature be in the Crown.

That each of the American Houses, may with the approbation of the Representitive of the Crown, elect two Commissioners to sit in the two Houses of the British Parliament, with the priviledge of Members so far as relate to representing and giving information of the Affairs and Circumstances of their Constituents; but without any right to vote or decide upon the question; and that the Parliament of Great Britain, have the like priviledge of sending two Commissioners to sit in the different Houses of the American branch.

In time of War, Bills for granting Aids to the Crown, may to prevent delay be finally passed into Laws by the Kings Representative, being Authorized by a temporary Act of Parliament.

The Jurisdiction of the American branch being confined to the general Affairs of America it will be necessary, and perhaps good policy, to give the Colonial Legislatures, the power of regulating their own respective and particular internal affairs, subject as usual to the Negative of the Crown.

The peace establishment of each Country exclusive of the Military may be maintained by itself. In America best by the Colonies. But the Aids to be granted to the Crown by the American branch, should be in proportion to the wealth of each Country. This proportion may be adjusted by a comparative view of the wealth of both.

The proportion of each Country being settled, it should be a fundamental stipulation in the compact of Union, that whenever Great Britain shall give   America shall give   and so in proportion to any greater or less sum given by Great Britain.

And as the wealth of one Country may increase more than that of the other, it may be further stipulated that when the Exports of either shall rise or fall the proportion of Aids shall rise or fall in the same proportion.

The appointment of all Governors, Judicial, Ministerial and executive Officers and Offices, as well those which concern the Administration of Justice, as the Collection receiving and paying out the public Revenues, and all Military Officers should remain in the Crown. In short the Royal prerogative should by no means be lessened or abridged by the Union, but be the same in both Countries.

All Acts of Assembly which affect the prerogative of the Crown should be declared void.

All the Governments of the several Colonies should be reduced to one form, and consist of a Governor and Privy Council to be appointed by the Crown, and to hold their Offices during pleasure, an upper house of the same appointment whose Members should hold their Offices during good behaviour and to be removeable on the joint address of the Governor and Assembly; and an Assembly chosen by the people.

That the Trade of the Colonies shall be navigated in the same manner, and subject to the same regulations and restrictions, and liable to the same Imposts and duties on every Article of foreign Growth produce and Manufacture imported into Great Britain; and that the money arising from the Imports and duties paid in America, be applied to their proportion of American Aids.

That the Colonies shall have the same privileges of exporting the Articles of their own Growth and produce, except such Articles as are necessary and wanting to support and carry on the Manufactures of Great Britain, and to furnish its Navy with Naval Stores. And that these Articles shall be imported into Great Britain only.

That all Acts of Parliament affecting the Colonies and inconsistent with the Principles of this Union be repealed.

That the General Statutes of the Realm and the Common Law be declared in Force in America, and that all Colonial Laws making any Alteration in Them, and all Others whatever shall be transmitted within Six Months to His Majesty in Council for his

Confirmation or Repeal, and that all Laws not so transmitted be void.

That Two Bishops resident in America be appointed, vested with Ecclesiastical Powers only, to superintend and manage the Affairs of the established Church, and confined to the Consecration of Churches and Ordination, Confirmation, and the Government of the Clergy belonging to their own Churches.

That the Bishops have a competent Salary to be paid out of the Quitrents, or the Revenues which may arise from Lands, now unlocated and to be appropriated for that Purpose.

That full Liberty of Conscience be tollerated in America, but that All General Ecclesiastical Committees, Assemblies and Synods, consisting of the Members of more Society's or Congregations than One, and All standing Conventions, Committees, Town Meetings and Associations not authorised by any Law, be declared unlawful and Siditious Assemblies and punishable by Fine, and Imprisonment. Provided that no one Occasional Meeting for the purpose of petitioning for any wanted Regulation, or a Redress of any Grievance, shall be deemed such unlawful Assembly.

That the Salaries of all the Officers of the Crown be ascertained and fixed. The Salary of the Lord Lieutenant to be paid out of the General Aids granted by the Colonies, and those of the Governor, Judges &c by a Colonial Grant.

Perhaps for many Reasons, it will be good Pollicy to divide the Colonies, into three following Districts, viz.:

Northern District	Middle District	Southern District
Canada	New York	North Carolina
Newfoundland	New Jersey	South Carolina
Nova Scotia	Pennsylvania	Georgia
New Hampshire	Delaware Counties	East Florida
Massachusetts	Maryland	West Florida
Connecticut	Virginia	
Rhode Island		

And to give to each the Constitution proposed in the foregoing Plan.

[The above plan I had the honour with Mr. Galloway to lay

before my Lord George Germain in March 1780;[2] and had it then been adopted, the Colonies would have now been united with Great Britain—I have the honour to be your Most Devoted Hum^{le}. Servt.

JOHN MORRISON

7 March 1788][3]

To the Right Honble

HENRY DUNDAS &c. &c. &c.

[2] The Galloway-Morrison Plan of Union of 1780, which is substantially the same as this one, is a seven-page document in the Stopford-Sackville MSS., the William L. Clements Library. See page 98, note 30.

[3] The part in brackets was obviously written at a later period than the remainder of the document.

INDEX

INDEX

Adams, John, 31; on nature of American Revolution, 4; on imperial constitution, 1, 9; *Novanglus Letters*, 10; on question of Parliamentary supremacy, 26, 27; accuses *JG* of Machiavellian dissimilation, 32; notes on *JG's* speech in Congress on Plan of Union, 35-36; appeals to John Locke, 47; on Franklin's opinion of de Weissenstein's Plan of Union, 79.

Adams, R. G., ix.

Adams, Samuel, 3, 12.

Albany Congress, 13, 19, 24; Plan of Union said to have influenced *JG*, 37.

Allen, William, 54; attacks *JG* in Penna. legislature, 50.

Americanus [JG], 21-22.

Amherst, Lord, confirms *JG's* census of Philadelphia, 83.

Amor Patriae, author of a Plan of Union, 25-26.

Arguments on Both Sides, written by *JG*, 33.

Baltimore, Lord, 88.

Bernard, Governor Francis, 25.

Bishops, American, proposed by *JG*, 96, 98.

Blackstone, Sir William, 3; definition of Parliamentary supremacy, 9-10; opposed by James Wilson, 12.

British Empire, threatened disruption of, 1, 6-7, 105; *JG's* ideas of rôle of colonies in, 55-56; *JG* on importance of trade and fisheries to, 73-74; mercantilist system, 106, 110; imperial defense, 106.

British ministry, attitude of, toward Loyalists, 76-77; attacked by *JG* for not prosecuting war vigorously, 72*ff.*

Bryan, George, 84.

Bucks County, proceedings of Committee of Safety in, 41-44.

Burgoyne, General John, attacked by *JG*, 74.

Burke, Edmund, cross-examines *JG*, 72.

Burlamaqui, J. J., 78.

Bute, Lord, 100, 101.

Camden, Lord, opinion of *JG's* Plan of Union, 38-39.

Canada, 98, 176; contrasted with United States, 8.

Candid Examination, by *JG*, attacks Continental Congress, 45-46; approved by conservatives, 48; burned and destroyed by "independents," 49.

Carleton, Sir Guy, 70.

Carlisle Commission, 70.

Carolina, Fundamental Constitutions of, 82.

Carpenter's Hall, 29.

Cawthorne, John Fenton, credited with authorship of Plan of Union, 79.

Chastellux, Marquis de, on legality of American Revolution, 12.

Chatham, Lord, opinion of *JG's* Plan of Union, 38-39.

Chester, 89, 90.

Christ Church, 22.

Circular Letter, Massachusetts, 22.

Clinton, George, suggests inter-colonial union, 13.

Clinton, Sir Henry, succeeds Howe, 70; advised not to trust, *JG*, 76-77; receives Plan of Union from Morrison, 94; gives Morrison permission to go to England, 96.

College of New Jersey, gives honorary degree to *JG*, 18-19.

Committee of Correspondence, *JG* drafts communication by, to Massachusetts, 32.

Committee of Safety, Bucks County, proceedings of, 41-44.

Congress, Continental, *JG* keeps Dickinson out of Pa. delegation to, 27; *JG* on delegates to, 28;

54359

DATE DUE

30 505 JOSTEN'S